Redeeming Flesh

Redeeming Flesh

The Way of the Cross with Zombie Jesus

Matthew John Paul Tan

CASCADE *Books* • Eugene, Oregon

REDEEMING FLESH
The Way of the Cross with Zombie Jesus

Cascade Books
An Imprint of Wipf and Stock Publishers
199 W. 8th Ave., Suite 3
Eugene, OR 97401

www.wipfandstock.com

PAPERBACK ISBN: 978-1-4982-9117-0
HARDCOVER ISBN: 978-1-4982-9119-4
EBOOK ISBN: 978-1-4982-9118-7

Cataloguing-in-Publication data:

Tan, Matthew John Paul.

Redeeming flesh : the way of the cross with zombie Jesus / Matthew John Paul Tan.

x + 100 pp. ; 23 cm. Includes bibliographical references and index.

ISBN 978-1-4982-9117-0 (paperback) | ISBN 978-1-4982 9119 4 (hardback) | ISBN 978-1-4982-9118-7 (ebook)

1. Zombies—Religious aspects—Christianity. 2. Zombie films—Religious aspects—Christianity. 3. Popular culture—Religious aspects—Christianity. 4. Zombies in literature—Religious aspects—Christianity. 5. Fear of death. I. Title.

BR115.C8 T36 2016

Manufactured in the U.S.A.   06/27/16

For Gregory Jordan SJ and the faithful departed

Christ is risen from the dead! By death He trampled
Death and to those in the tombs He granted life.

—A Paschal Troparion

Table of Contents

Acknowledgements

THIS BOOK BEGAN ITS life as a Holy Week retreat I gave in 2015, at the kind invitation of Father Paul Chandler O. Carm, spiritual director of Holy Spirit Seminary in the Archdiocese of Brisbane in Australia. It was through facilitating that retreat and through my engagement with the seminarians that this book has become possible. It is to them that I owe my thanks.

I

Introduction

WHAT IS PRESENTED HERE is part speculative theology, part social critique, and part devotional, focusing on the trope of the zombie. The launch point of this work will be "Zombie Jesus," which centers on the whimsical claim that Jesus, having exhorted all to eat his flesh and risen from the dead, was history's first zombie. "Zombie Jesus" first emerged as an exclamation by one of the characters, Hubert J. Farnsworth, in an episode of the Matt Groening animated TV series *Futurama* in 1999 entitled "When Aliens Attack." Though the character himself was not shown in *Futurama*, "Zombie Jesus" has since become immortalized in a smorgasbord of memes, comedy skits, and zombie walks around the world. In this inquiry, "Zombie Jesus" will act as a touchstone for a broader inquiry into the reasons behind the prominence of the zombie in popular culture, and how the Christian might engage the motif of the zombie at a cultural level, in light of its popularity among Christian and non-Christian consumers of popular culture alike. This work will also highlight how the Christian might engage the zombie at a *theological* level, and make the zombie not only a part of his or her consumption of popular culture, but also a way towards cultivating a greater appreciation of the saving work of God.

Readers might wonder how anyone can yield anything of theological, or even devotional, significance from something as whimsical as a zombie. Indeed, readers might even be scandalized at the thought that anything of benefit to the spiritual life can be gained from the meme of "Zombie Jesus," especially when one considers that the meme was initially used to poke fun at Christianity's assertion of the centrality of the resurrection and Jesus' injunction to eat his flesh as the indispensable means to have eternal life.[1] In and of itself, the "Zombie Jesus" meme might be at worst offensive to those within the Christian fold, or at best amusing to those outside it. Even at its best, however, we may feel that the meme does not provide any great cultural, let alone theological, insight. It is submitted here, however, that "Zombie Jesus" can be a useful launch point into a more comprehensive investigation of the zombie as a pop cultural phenomenon, a phenomenon that now incorporates into its purview movies, television series, video games, and even nineteenth-century Gothic literature.

This study will incorporate some elements of this phenomenon, but also highlight its cultural salience with reference to other practices within pop culture more generally. The inquiry will then widen to integrate the insights into the zombie gleaned by cultural theory and theology. It will argue that, with the aid of the former, "Zombie Jesus" can act as an endpoint of a highly potent social critique that has the zombie as an indispensable touchstone. The book will show how the monstrosity of the zombie is not a bizarre category that sits outside the warp and woof of material culture, but is an integral part of that culture. In other words, material culture is indeed monstrous and there lurks in postmodern culture a death of flesh that parallels that of the flesh of the zombie. This book will also assert, however, that the aid of the latter can afford this inquiry something more than a mere critique of the material processes of a pop cultural form. This is important since confining the inquiry to critique risks merely describing the way that cultural form functions and even reifying and reinforcing its practices, institutions, and semiotics. The inclusion of theology into an investigation into a zombie meme will hopefully serve two important purposes. The first is to highlight the possibilities of the discipline of not only speculating on the things transcendent, but

1. John 6:53.

also in making unique contributions to immanent critique. In doing so, this work hopes to highlight aspects of the yearnings that swirl within pop cultural forms that pop cultural analysis might miss. Secondly, it is hoped that integrating both theology and immanent critique will also highlight the highly visceral operations of the economy of salvation, of Christ's role in that economy, and of the effects of that role on the reader. For Christ's saving work is not merely operative at the level of the emotions or even at some vague "spiritual" level. Christ saved, the Gospel of John remind us, by taking on our *flesh*[2] and, as the incarnate Word, Christ saved also by taking on the *futility* of our flesh, a point made in Paul's letter to the Romans.[3] Thus, the saving action of Christ not only gives life in an abstract sense, but also "gives life to your mortal bodies,"[4] at the level of our flesh and through the action of his own flesh.

In order to substantiate this claim, this book will be structured as three inquiries. In order to better appreciate the cultural potency of the zombie in the West, the first inquiry will look at the genealogy of the zombie from its entry into the literature of the anglosphere in the mid-eighteenth century to the present day. This particular inquiry will show how the stage was set for the zombie's entry into our imagination through the writings of the "Graveyard Poets," with their focus on death and the grave, as the name suggests. It will show how the dead, and later the undead, were not merely instruments for our humor, but functioned as a form of critique on the welfare of souls. Whether such a critique succeeded is debatable, but what is beyond debate is a legacy of cementing the motif of death—and our ability to come to grips with death—in the popular imagination. This first inquiry will also show how, far from disappearing in the so called "Age of the Enlightenment," critique through the motif of death lingered on in Gothic literature in the more familiar forms of the undead, and

2. John 1:14.

3. "For creation was subjected to futility, not willingly, but because of him who subjected it" (Rom 8:20).

4. Rom 8:11.

continued on well into the twentieth century, in what is known as the "Romero Zombie," named after the movies *Night of the Living Dead*[5] and *Dawn of the Dead*,[6] directed by George Romero. This genealogical exploration will then take the inquiry into the zombie in the direction of an immanent critique, a "Zombie-*Kritik*" if you will. Here, the book will consider the literature that looks to the zombie as a critique of modern metaphysics and postmodern culture as well as a warning of where that lifeworld might end up if these conditions persisted. This aspect of the inquiry will be by no means exhaustive, but will merely highlight key observations. In making this critique, the book will submit that the spectacle of the zombie is not just another whimsical artifact of a public fascination with horror, nor is the zombie a mere monster fundamentally set apart from the viewer of the spectacle. Rather, the focusing of social and cultural theory onto the zombie will show the extent to which the monstrosity of the zombie is actually a reflection of the consumer culture that produced it. The book will suggest that the zombie is not just the endpoint of the urge to consume that which swirls within pop culture. The act of consumption is also part of a project within postmodern culture to create a meeting point between heaven and earth, a site of what Bruno Latour calls "alternation between transcendence and immanence." With reference to what Freudian psychoanalysis calls the "death drive"—and what the Slovenian Marxist Slavoj Žižek more pointedly calls "undeadness"—this part of the inquiry will explore how postmodern culture creates an amalgam of transcendence and immanence by enlisting the very flesh of the consumer, molding that flesh into the flesh of a "postmodern angel," to borrow the terminology of Graham Ward. Whilst an angel may not sound anywhere near as grotesque as the zombie, this chapter will nonetheless show how, at a metaphysical as well as a cultural level, it is the very process of transforming ordinary flesh into the angelic that leads to the death of all flesh.

5. Romero, *Night of the Living Dead* (1968).

6. Romero, *Dawn of the Dead* (1978).

Vital though this critical inquiry may be, this work argues that there are aspects of the zombie—and by extension, the practices within the pop cultural form—that get missed in an investigation using social theory alone. Given the limitations of the first inquiry in isolation, a second inquiry will seek to highlight some of these blind spots by enlisting the aid of the discipline of theology. The aim of the decidedly theological nature of this second inquiry is twofold. First, it hopes to highlight aspects of immanent critique that might be missed even by immanent critique itself. It will do this by juxtaposing an indispensable characterization of the zombie—the flesh-eating horde—with two important theological categories, namely ecclesiology (a theory of the church) and liturgy (a theory of public worship). With the former, this book will show how the act of gathering provides a means of explaining the potency of the zombie, not at an individual level, but at the level of the collective. It will show how the zombie is defined not by virtue of its individuality, but by virtue of its collectivity. This book will show how, even if the act of gathering might be canvassed in the coverage of the *phenomenon* of the zombie, that phenomenon nonetheless betrays a lingering yearning for a collective identity, even if that identity threatens to overwhelm or erase the individual subject. This is not only done as a way to articulate one's identity as an identity shaped by others, but also as a way to articulate the means by which one is *saved* by others. This salvific aspect of incorporation into a collectivity is expressed as a zombified form of ecclesiology which can only be deciphered and critically engaged by means of a theological grammar. It will show how ecclesiology can assist in understanding the zombie, not only in terms of a crude collectivity, but also in evaluating the success with which that collective relates to and harmonizes with the particularity of individual bodies.

As shall also be seen, ecclesiology will dovetail into a consideration of liturgy. The book will highlight how the act of consuming flesh by a zombie horde has parallels to another act of consuming flesh by a collective, one that is done in churches across the world—the Eucharistic liturgy. It is precisely at this juncture that the flesh of the zombie comes into contact with the Word made flesh and the remainder of the book will consider the trope of the zombie through the lens of the Eucharist. It will be at this Eucharistic juncture where the monstrosity of the zombie is fully revealed. However, the book will also show how that very monstrosity becomes undone by a Eucharistic logic. Monstrosity is overcome, not by plastering over the rotting flesh of the zombie, but by incorporating the dying flesh of the horde into the living flesh in the body of Christ. This joining of flesh is undertaken, not by a divine erasure of the "death drive," but by a divine *entry* into it, redirecting it. The Eucharist will thus act as the vital touchstone in our main assertion—that the grammar of the saving work of Christ is brought about not through a violent overcoming of the zombie, but by Christ himself taking on the condition of a zombie, giving flesh, so to speak, to the line by St. Paul, who talks of Christ as "he who knew no sin [and] became sin on our behalf."[7] This line of inquiry makes the Eucharist a vital element because it highlights how Christ takes on the zombified condition by handing over his flesh to be consumed by the horde. Nevertheless, it is precisely because it is Eucharistic that the consumption of his flesh only becomes a prelude to an absorption of that zombified flesh into his living body.

Having laid out the contours of a Eucharistic engagement with the zombie, the third and final inquiry will show how this salvific process of consumption by Christ, is not merely another bizarre foray into the sometimes hermetically sealed world of postmodern theology. This final inquiry will take the analyses of the previous two inquiries out into the texture of spiritual devotion, and integrate the theoretical reflections drawn from social theory and theology with the spiritual reflections of the medieval devotion of the Stations of the Cross (sometimes called "The Way of the Cross"), albeit in truncated form. Through the Way of the Cross this book will highlight how, in the passion of Christ, Jesus assumes the zombified condition of his condemners, torturers, executioners, and even the bystanders. In the Stations the reader will

7. 2 Cor 5:21.

be shown the sheer gravity of the zombified condition that Jesus takes on, a condition signified by the cross he must bear and to which he must be bound. The Stations will also highlight, however, the spectre of the death of flesh, but will do so through the way in which that death of flesh comes in the form of a Eucharistic distribution, a distribution that also gives life to the zombified. Thus, while the Way of the Cross depicts a seemingly inexorable path to Golgotha, it will also depict a path whereby the flesh handed over for consumption gives way at several crucial junctures to a redeeming of zombified flesh through its contact with—and eventual absorption by—the living body of the Lord.

2

The Zombie Is Us

Introduction

THE FIRST TASK OF this book is to locate its central inquiry within a broader literature of the undead as a pop cultural icon. Thus, it will be necessary to outline the kinds of critiques that are leveled at contemporary culture via the trope of the zombie. In order to do this, this chapter will briefly examine two analytical threads concerning the zombie. It will first look at the genealogy of the zombie, since a genealogical analysis highlights important differences at each stage of the development of the zombie to the form that we currently know. (It is important to note that the zombie of contemporary pop culture is only a very recent manifestation.) A genealogical analysis will also be able to highlight the peculiarities of each stage of the development, as well as identify any factors that might lead to a subsequent development. What should become apparent in the course of outlining this genealogy is a link between the development of the zombie motif, changes in social attitudes to theological categories, and subsequent changes to their outward social institutionalizations. More specifically, it should become apparent that the zombie as it has developed within the Anglosphere was intended as a device for critiquing particular ways of life, as well as affirmations of certain social aspirations.

Having done the genealogical spadework and highlighting the crucial cultural and theological developments, the next task of the chapter will be to outline what the cultural ascendency of the zombie within recent years in popular culture says about the culture we currently inhabit. This will take the form of an immanent critique with the zombie acting as the foil. This "Zombie-*Kritik*" will expose not only a societal urge to consume things but also a communal longing to produce something angelic through the consumption of things and, in doing so, create a form of heaven on earth.

Zombie Genealogy

When one's media consumption has been overrun with the zombies in *World War Z*, *The Walking Dead*, *28 Days* and *Weeks Later*, and *Shaun of the Dead*, one might be forgiven for thinking that zombies have always taken the form of the mindless flesh-eating corpse. In what follows, however, it will be shown that the zombie familiar to popular culture today is actually of a very recent vintage, a blip within a rather complex genealogy that exposes many permutations.

The complexity of the zombie's genealogy becomes apparent when one looks at the word "zombie" itself. The term "zombie" does not derive from English, but rather the Haitian creole word *zonbi*, an indicator that Haiti is where the zombie's origins are found. The zombie in the rural folklore of Haiti bears only a little resemblance to the undead type we are familiar with today. There are versions of the folklore that involve a fully alive human that falls under the control of a witch doctor or *bokor*, a slave that is fully alive but who has completely lost his or her free will. However, it is more common within the folklore that the *bokor* is engaged in necromancy, the raising of those that are already dead to serve as the slaves of the *bokor*. In both circumstances, the *zonbi* is depicted as a slave under the control of another.

With the zombie's entry into the literature of the Anglosphere, one sees a decisive turn in its evolution in the popular imagination.

The story of the zombie's development in the Anglosphere begins with the convergence of two early to mid-eighteenth-century literary threads. The first of these threads might at first blush be too subtle to be a contributing factor to the emergence of the zombie as we know it. It constitutes a set of pre-Romantic poets known as the "Graveyard Poets," incorporating figures such as Thomas Parnell, William Collins, and Joseph Warton. These poets were not engaged in writing about reanimated corpses as such. However, "Graveyard Poetry" as a genre was largely responsible for turning the popular attention towards things pertaining to the dead, namely the grave, death, bereavement, and the occasional ghost. While not talking about the revivification of the dead, the fact that the genre drew the popular imagination to the dead alone makes it a highly significant literary development.

However, "Graveyard Poetry" is also important for two other more fundamental reasons, according to the entertainment historian Walter Kendrick. The first is that this relatively obscure eighteenth-century genre laid the foundations for the more familiar genre of Gothic literature in the nineteenth century, which, unlike the former, did explicitly use the trope of the reanimated corpse. The second reason—one that is more tantalizing considering the central hypothesis of a book focusing on the relation between the zombie and theology—is that the "Graveyard Poets" were, for the most part, clergymen. This historical quirk sheds new light on the genre's attention to the things of the dead. A Graveyard Poet is not merely being morbid by casting a reader's attention towards the grave. Rather, in fulfilling the function of a Christian clergymen, the drawing of one's mind towards death was only a precursor to a call for a reader's *repentance* to God in the face of the reader's *own* impending death. This at first seems to compound the severity of drawing the reader's attention to death, by suggesting that escaping one form of oppression is only possible by subjecting oneself to another. However, what is important to note that the "Graveyard Poets" often coupled the morbidity of death with a hopeful note. This note can be summarized in terms of God's mercy, which cuts through the finality of death, even as the genre recognized that death is a monstrous interruption to life. While "the effects of death are horrible" there is a comfort that immortality beyond the grave can redeem that monstrosity.[1]

The "Graveyard Poets" thus had firmly in their sights the Christian God, and thus the Christian trope of mercy and hope beyond the grave. The evolution of the zombie would take a more ominous turn, however, around the time that the philosophies of the Enlightenment emerged. Although not exactly a new development in intellectual history,[2] the Enlightenment period historically marked the most decisive turn away from religious faith as a source and foundation of reasoning, to a more secular reason grounded in technical prowess. It was a secular reasoning both in terms of its disengagement from acts of faith, and in terms of its proclaimed universality of application. This secular reasoning was deemed to be superior to the faith-based reasoning that came before it and deemed to bear greater capacities for a fully immanent salvation of mankind—a salvation that depended not on an arbitrary divine intervention but on the readily available and reliable stores of human effort. At a cultural level, this form of salvation was celebrated under the banner of the inexorable progress of civilization. Strange as it may seem, this largely intellectual shift in the nineteenth century will also have a bearing on the evolution in Anglosphere literature on the dead. More specifically, the decisive turn away from religious foundations of knowledge in the West is not lost on Kendrick, who noted a parallel between the shift brought about by the Enlightenment, and the literary shift from the dead to the undead. Kendrick regards the emergence of the undead as a literary manifestation of "the twisted memory of lost faith [which] haunts us still." With that loss of trust in faith as a firm foundation of reasoning, comes "our culture's loss of trust in redemption."[3] Kendrick regards the undead as a literary expression

---

1. Kendrick, *In the Thrill of Fear*, 31.

2. John Milbank, for instance, argues that the roots of separating faith from reason can be found in the medieval thought of Duns Scotus. See Milbank, *Theology and Social Theory*.

3. Kendrick, *In the Thrill of Fear*, 32.

of a cultural anxiety. This is an anxiety that, having collectively lost faith in God and in any hope of redemption beyond the grave, mankind lives under an ominous shadow and is doomed only to wait to be overwhelmed by that shadow.

This anxiety generated by the loss of the expectation of that redemptive moment can be seen in the next stage in the evolution of the zombie: the trope of the reanimated corpse in nineteenth-century Gothic fiction. The link between the reanimated corpse and the civilizational anxiety over the loss of that redemptive moment is twofold. First, in the reanimated corpse, immortality folds back on itself and brings a modicum of eternal life to that which is already—and still—dead. Secondly, and this compounds the horror of seeing the dead return, the return of the corpse is coupled by its turning on the living in a vengeful fashion. Arguably the earliest and probably most famous example of this genre in the popular imagination is Mary Shelley's 1819 work, *Frankenstein*. The only qualification to this, however, is that the monster was manufactured and its reanimation was by design. Thus, *Frankenstein* can be more accurately described as articulating the anxiety of the scientific manipulation of nature backfiring, a variant of the anxieties generated by the Enlightenment. Other notable but less famous Gothic works, however, express that more familiar anxiety surrounding the zombie, whereby the corpse comes back from the dead without human intervention. This finds its expression in Gothic literature in the vein of Edgar Allen Poe's *The Fall of the House of Usher*, which was first published in 1839. In Poe's work a buried girl, Madeleine Usher, returns from the grave and tries to kill her twin brother, Roderick. The return of the previously interred Madeleine to take her brother back to the grave with her is indeed monstrous, expressing that post-Enlightenment anxiety of that loss of redemption. What is interesting particularly in Poe's work, however, is that the author leaves open to the reader the possibility of inferring that the attack was the fault of the victim, Roderick. In the book itself, Roderick says that Madeleine may have been buried alive, though the truth of this is qualified by the fact that Roderick suffers from an unnamed psychological ailment.

Though there is no clear evidence, a number of literary critics have also hinted at the possibility that the attack on Roderick could be vengeance for an incestuous relationship between him and Madeleine.[4] Whatever the cause, the point Poe seemed to indicate is that the living somehow deserved the vengeful attack.

In the final years of the nineteenth century, one witnesses another turn on the Gothic theme of the reanimated corpse. Instead of attacking in an act of vengeance against the guilty, as it was in Poe's work, the dead reanimate and attack the innocent as well. This idea, however, is manifested in another distinctly recognizable form of the undead, namely the vampire of Bram Stoker's *Dracula* (1897). It is at this point where the monstrosity of the undead is intensified, for this manifestation of the undead not only turns on the living. It also feeds on the living and spreads the condition of undeadness to its victims, exponentially increasing the threat to the living as time goes on. Here again, as Susannah Clements argues in *The Vampire Defanged*, in *Dracula* one sees a highly explicit nod to the religious faith left behind by the West. Indeed, Clements notices that *Dracula* does more than most to mine the idiosyncrasies of the Christian heritage to extol its virtues, claiming that Bram Stoker's vampire invokes the theological trope of sin and its consequent powers to seduce a person to his or her own perdition. This is a threat from which the cross—often used to repel vampires—saves.[5] The recovery of the discussion of sin and *its* seductive (and destructive) power was, however, brief. As *Dracula* faded from the public imagination, so too did the consideration of the destructive power of sin. Indeed, Clements notes how with this muting of the discussion of sin, the vampire over the decades evolved from being the malevolent force of *Dracula*, to the alluring object of sexual desire as embodied in Edward of Stephanie Meyer's *Twilight* series of vampire novels. With the disappearance of the vampire as a threat to mankind, there also seemed little incentive to give any weight to that hopeful glimmer of redemption from that threat.

4. Wasserman, "The Self, the Mirror, the Other," 33.

5. Clements, *The Vampire Defanged*, 13–32.

What did endure in the public imagination, however, was the trope of the reanimated corpse that feeds on the living, and spreading the condition of undeadness to others. As the twentieth century progressed, and as the main medium of popular culture shifted from books to film, this trope would come full circle and loop back onto the zombie mentioned at the beginning of our genealogy. This looping back would occur in the mid-twentieth century, with the release of the 1968 film *Night of the Living Dead* and the sequel *Dawn of the Dead* in 1978, by George Romero. It is to Romero that contemporary fans of the zombie owe their thanks, since it is he who created the zombie with which they would be familiar. What is significant about the emergence of the "Romero Zombie," as Kim Paffenroth points out, is that at this point, the divide between the dead and the living starts to blur. While the reanimated corpse motif remains, it is unlike the Dracula that came before it in a number of very important respects. First, recall that Dracula possesses superhuman capabilities such as flight, shape-shifting, and even powers of seduction. Apart from having returned from the dead, the zombie, unlike Dracula, possesses no extraordinary capabilities and remains human, at least in a sense, retaining all the characteristics of human embodiment, including the ghastly effects of bodily decay. Secondly, while the vampire exhibits levels of intelligence that may even surpass human capabilities, zombies are mere shells of the persons they once were. Indeed, what distinguishes zombies from other forms of the undead is that they retain only the most basic brain functions, and thus only act upon their basest human instincts, most particularly on the instinct to feed. Third, while the vampire attacks by draining the body of blood, the zombie attacks by devouring the body itself, and very often leaving mangled masses of flesh behind. Fourth, while the threat posed by the vampire is usually on a one-on-one basis, the zombies' main threat comes from their sheer force of numbers, and their rapid multiplication through a simple bite, however slight, creating a tsunami of flesh-feeding that eventually consumes mankind.[6] In the "Romero-zombie" we see the post-Enlightenment anxiety of

6. Paffenroth, "Apocalyptic Images," 147.

irredeemability reach a crescendo, as both the good and the bad perish at the hands and teeth of monsters for no apparent reason. Moreover, their monstrosity arises not from extraordinary super-human capabilities, but from the fact that they are driven by nothing more than the most basic human drives.

It is noteworthy that the popularity of the Romero-zombie is overtaking, if it has not already overtaken, the popularity of another undead already mentioned, namely the vampire. In the half-century since Romero's two famous movies, a huge range of zombie-related media have been released across many different platforms. Film remains the dominant medium, with variants of the zombie theme including *Shaun of the Dead, Fido, Warm Bodies, 28 Days Later* and its sequel *28 Weeks Later*, five adaptations of the game series *Resident Evil*[7] and, most recently, the movie *World War Z* being the most prominent examples, although there are more than sixty popular zombie movies in circulation. In video gaming, zombies have also proven highly popular with games like Capcom's *Resident Evil* franchise and Naughty Dog's *The Last of Us*, which won hundreds of "game of the year" awards from gaming publications. Arguably, the popularity of the "Romero-zombie" is best represented by the AMC television series *The Walking Dead*, which at the time of writing is in its sixth season. An indicator of the popularity of the series can be found in the first episode of the third season of the series, which received the statistical accolade of being the most watched television episode in the history of cable television. The popularity of the series has prompted the generation of other zombie-themed television series, such as Channel 4 mini-series *Dead Set* and the BBC mini-series *In the Flesh*, the

---

7. It must be noted that *28 Days Later, 28 Weeks Later*, and the *Resident Evil* series of movies adapt the motif of the reanimated corpse, involving instead the motif of the virally infected living human. Though at the surface, this variation may break the continuity of the zombie as the reanimated corpse, the motif of the infected human has the same effect on the subject in that, in the absence of a cure, the complexity of the human subject permanently gives way to the base instinct to attack and feed. Indeed, it can be argued that, because the virus is of human origin, it brings into the zombie the post-Enlightenment anxieties concerning the capacity of scientific manipulation to backfire.

driver of which is the premise that being a zombie is a condition that can be cured, though it is revealed that the divisions caused by the physical disease are dwarfed by the social divisions generated by the cure.

The above genealogy is by no means comprehensive, but what it hopefully hints at is that the emergence and evolution of the zombie, while in itself fascinating, is bound up together with shifts in the commitments, aspirations, and anxieties embedded within particular societal forms. This coupling may be somewhat obscured in the act of watching a zombie and, depending on one's proclivity to zombies, either wincing in horror or laughing with ridicule. However, what binds these differing reactions is the tendency to treat the zombie as a creature that is diametrically opposed to the human being, even if it does share more physical commonalities than previous versions of the undead. In spite of this apparent difference, however, the next section will demonstrate how the "Romero Zombie" was actually intended to function as a cinematic version of what the philosophers of the Frankfurt School called *Kulturkritik*, a critical investigation that mines the presumptions embedded within the practices and institutions of contemporary Western culture, which we regard as natural givens. This section will show that while Romero is nowhere near as sophisticated as the Frankfurt School in his final analysis within the films themselves, the "Romero Zombie" not only reflects but also critiques the kinds of cultures we live in, the practices that make them up, and the persons that undertake those practices.

Zombie-*Kritik*: The Urge to Consume

The uncontrollable drive of the zombie to consume the living is an understandable point of horror for the movie viewer. Be that as it may, that very consumption is the linchpin on which Romero's critique hangs, as such a drive to consume by the undead acts as a mirror of the drive for *humans* to consume within modern societies. Thus, the very act that is meant to distinguish the human from the zombie actually becomes the liminal space in which those very differences give way to similarities. This liminality is most pointedly made in Romero's 1978 film *Dawn of the Dead*, where a gigantic shopping mall serves as the central backdrop to a major standoff between survivors and zombies. A number of points come through in this movie that deserve detailed consideration.

The first and most explicit parallel that is drawn is the way in which the zombies depicted in the movie congregate around the mall, even before the arrival of the human survivors. When asked why this is the case one of the survivors, Peter, remarks that the zombies feel drawn to the mall because the experiences of the mall had somehow imprinted themselves onto their living predecessors as "an important place in their lives," even more so, Kim Paffenroth notes, than the churches, libraries, and the classrooms in the movie, all of which are noticeably less crowded with zombies.[8] This acute attribution of importance to the mall became so hardwired and primordial that, upon death, being at the mall remains within the zombie as a basic instinct.[9] Indeed, the hardwiring of the mall into the zombie has become so primordial that the urge to enter these sites of consumption eclipses any concern for their welfare as they do so. Romero thereby blurs the mindless consumption of human flesh by the zombie with the mindless consumption of products in the mall, and the mall becomes mapped out onto the zombies.

Romero also extends the mapping out of the mall onto the human person to the living. For the survivors, once safe in the mall, gradually indulge themselves with the products within the mall. This indulgence leads to what Loudermilk calls a "Mall Fantasia," a kind of *ennui* that sets in which is set off by the easy access to a swathe of ultimately useless products, such as jewelry, fashions, and cosmetics.[10] It is at this point where Romero begins to draw uncomfortable parallels between humans and zombies. In the same way that the zombie is unconcerned about its own welfare in satisfying the urge to consume, "Mall Fantasia" is a

8. Paffenroth, "Apocalyptic Images," 153.

9. Ibid.

10. Loudermilk, "Eating 'Dawn,'" 92–93.

kind of deadening of the desire to escape the clear and present danger of zombies that slowly break their way into the mall and, in doing so, live. This is expressed by one of the survivors, Fran, when she warns another survivor about the mall with the words, "You're so hypnotized by this place, all of you. It's so bright and neatly wrapped you don't see that it's a prison too."[11] Paffenroth is more explicit when he says that a zombie's bite is unnecessary for turning a human into a zombie, since it is "materialism and consumerism that turns [humans] into zombies" as people become "addicted to things that satisfy only the basest, most animal or mechanical urges of our being."[12]

The second point concerns a strange inverse of this *ennui*, in that this deadening of desire brought about by superabundance manifests itself in an aggressive drive to consume as if one is engaged in a warfare over scarce commodities. In a way, this is not surprising since, as Steven Shaviro noted, such a condition of want "is a function of excess and extravagance, not of scarcity." Furthermore, the act of consumption does not assuage the urge to consume, but only makes that urge grow to more insatiable proportions. This is summed up by Shaviro with the phrase "the more I consume, the more I demand to consume."[13] This is demonstrated in a portion of the movie where the mall gets raided by a group of well-armed bandits, who fall into the aggressive inverse of *ennui*. Instead of wallowing in the wealth, like the survivors, the bandits, after fighting their way into the mall and creating a breach that the zombies exploit, do more than acquire the essentials for survival. Indeed, a battle ensues between the survivors and the bandits over the acquisition of jewelry and money. The survivor that begins the gun battle with the bandits justifies the action, not on the basis of the materiel's importance for their survival—much of the materials in the mall were not—but on the basis that the survivors were the first to acquire it. In the course of the acquisition frenzy over trinkets and the resultant battle over them, the bandits wind up

11. Ibid., 93.

12. Paffenroth, "Apocalyptic," 153.

13. Shaviro, *The Cinematic Body*, 92.

forsaking their own survival in the process, choosing to worsen the breach they created by fighting the survivors rather than co-operating with them. Eventually, they eventually succumb to the survivors and the zombies in the mall, and the mall is rendered useless for anyone as a hideout.

It is debatable whether Romero is successful in his critique of our consumer practices in films like *Dawn*, particularly the notion that the zombie is the sinister mirror-image of the human urge to consume, and that the distinction between the humans that consume things and the zombies that consume flesh can be blurred. This blurring may be somewhat undermined by the fact that, in the end, the viewer ends up hoping for the survivors to go on resisting the zombie onslaught. As Loudermilk also observes, it is questionable the degree to which Romero succeeds in critiquing consumer culture when he relied on that very culture to disseminate his films and thus his critique of consumerism.[14] Nevertheless, the substance of the critique itself endures. It is also possible to look at the zombie as more than a critique of consumerism. This point becomes especially acute when one considers that the urge to consume is but the end point of crucial social shifts and metaphysical developments taking place over centuries. It is to these matters, insofar as they relate to the trope of the zombie, that the critique now turns.

Zombie-*Kritik*: Death in the City of Angels

Angelic Flesh

This second thread begins with the remark made by Gary Laderman that the zombie is the "dark side of the luminous angels, while angels are eternally alive though disembodied, these zombie cannibals are eternally dead yet fully embodied."[15] The critique at this level looks beyond the phenomenon of consumption and tries to understand the *a priori* material and cultural processes and

14. Loudermilk, "Eating 'Dawn,'" 95.
15. Laderman, *Rest in Peace*, 123.

practices that work behind, stoke, and maintain the drive to consume. In order to do this, it is necessary to look beyond consumer culture as an abstract tag, but also interrogate the practices which make that culture a reality. The zombie then will become analyzed as the endpoint of these practices, manifesting their operations and unarticulated meanings.

To investigate these institutions, practices, and processes, it is necessary to first investigate the city. This is because the city is the most prominent backdrop against which the zombie, if not lives, certainly moves and has its being. With few exceptions, the "Romero Zombie" is an extension of the city in the same way as the mall around which the zombies congregate in *Dawn of the Dead*. In *The Walking Dead*, a number of episodes of the zombie drama may take place in rural settings, but such settings seem to only accentuate the reliance of the living on the products of city life and manufacturing, such as fuel, vehicles, communications equipment, industrial chemicals, medicines, machinery, or weaponry. More than a whole season is dedicated to the survivors eking out a living in an abandoned prison, which briefly becomes a site for the restoration of their former lives in the city. Although Rick, the leader of the group, dabbles in a new life of farming, the day-to-day running of the prison is dependent upon scavenging for materials in the nearby urban and suburban centers. The prison is eventually lost through a combination of zombie infestations from within, and a battle with a rival community from without. This battle results in the loss of that latter community, the prison, and with that the little oasis of normality as zombies eventually overtake the compound.

The use of the prison in a rural area as the focal point of this phase of the series is both poignant and relevant to our consideration of the city. Indeed, the prison can be considered a throwback of the city life that was lost when the zombie apocalypse occurred. Consider first the prison's rural location, often the result not of deliberate preference, but due to the planning priorities of city council planners and the sensitivity of their constituents to NIMBYs (Not-In-My-BackYard), and the resultant drive to banish institutions like the prison to the outer limits of the urban landscape.

Differences in locale notwithstanding, it is possible to further interrogate this relationship between the city and the prison not as diametric opposites, but as two subsets of the same lifeworld. This can be gleaned from a brief consideration of Michel Foucault's *Discipline and Punish*. Foucault suggests that, rather than the prison being an institution that stands in diametric opposition to what the city stands for, the city as we currently experience it emerged out of the same economy of technologies that gave birth to the modern prison. In other words, the city is a prison turned inside out, designed to give the illusion of freedom for the individual to do whatever he or she wants, while at the same time producing what Foucault called "docile bodies" for emerging forms of industrial and military organization.[16] What is suggested here is that cities and zombies share an intimate link worthy of interrogation and none should not be surprised that a growth in interest in the undead takes place against the backdrop of the growth of the postmodern city in the West and the astronomic growth of urban concentration around the world, with more people living in fewer and larger urban centres.

The parallel between the growth of cities as a form of social organization and the rise of the zombie in popular culture should not surprise, for cities are not just neutral infrastructure facilitating movement, with the lines and mounds of concrete, bitumen, and paint having no cultural, political, or even philosophical weight. Indeed, the twentieth-century Swiss architect Le Corbusier wrote in 1925 that "the layout of a city determines the physical and mental condition of its residents."[17] T. J. Gorringe went further to observe that "wittingly or unwittingly every design for council estates, every barrio, every skyscraper, every out of town supermarket, expresses a view of the human, embodies an ethic."[18] The city not only facilitates human movement in a neutral or passive manner, but also is a means of structuring and controlling movement and sight, bringing things into our vision and obscuring

16. Foucault, *Discipline and Punish*, 135–230.

17. Cited in Guiton, *The Ideas of Le Corbusier*, 94.

18. Gorringe, *A Theology of the Built Environment*, ix.

them from our line of sight, subtly making suggestions as to the objects, monuments, signs, and people we should interact with and invest ourselves in. More importantly, they articulate aspirations and cultural horizons.[19] With every road laid down or building erected, aspirations for the human condition are being made. Indeed, cities are the foundations on which utopias are built. But these utopic horizons are not secular, in that these horizons are not completely free of any smuggled theological claim.

In speaking of the urban planning of Ebenezer Howard, Graham Ward observes that in striving towards utopic horizons, one place seems to figure largely—the Garden of Eden. This is not accidental for Ward, nor is it confined to Howard's "Garden City Movement" of planning, in which urban centres are integrated into zones of greenery and foliage. Ward seems to suggest that cities in general, in articulating their cultural aspirations in their infrastructure, are also projections of Edenic states of perfection, where perfection is characterized by the unencumbered pursuit of leisure.[20] Such states of perfection that are to be found in cities and their accoutrements abound in popular culture. They are alluded to in the romance of songs like Dionne Warwick's *Do You Know the Way to San Jose* (even as the songs speak of escape from a larger city to another, albeit smaller, city), Lionel Ritchie's *All Night Long*, and Tracey Chapman's *Fast Car*, where the lyrics express longings for states of bliss in which one can live, love, party, and find fulfillment of one's wildest dreams, and a state akin to immortality has been attained. Interestingly, even elements of Contemporary Christian Music have not been oblivious to this link between the city and heavenly bliss. The Australian Christian music band Newsboys have as part of their repertoire a song entitled *Love Liberty Disco,* in which the halls of heaven are portrayed as an urban discotheque, with the redeemed dancing forever in a shower of multicolored lights and 1970s fashions. What can be gleaned here is that, in projecting states of perfection with every building, park, and highway, the city is, in the words of the historian Lewis

19. Mumford, *The City in History*, 42.

20. Ward, *Cities of God*, 38.

Mumford, representing "the cosmos, a means of bringing heaven down to earth."[21] This wording is suggestive, for it reemphasizes the states of immortality associated with the city. At the same time, however, the desire to bring heaven to earth suggests that what the city is striving for is not the heaven of the book of Revelation, in which the states of perfection described are subject to a timetable set by a transcendent God. What is sought instead is a city that strives for human perfection according to a *human* timetable. The city thus becomes, to borrow from the urban developer Philip Kasinitz, the site where God becomes dethroned and human genius leading to utopia is embodied.[22] The religious significance of seemingly "secular" urban buildings, in particular skyscrapers, was not lost on architects like Le Corbusier, who once gave the skyscrapers of New York the title of "new white cathedrals."[23] Thus, while the city strives to bring heaven down to earth, the heaven being brought down is a godless heaven, with humanity occupying pride of place. However, Ward notes that while these lofty expressions are being generated by the city, there is another, more ominous spectre being projected at the same time. Like the Frankenstein monster of Gothic literature, the city, in exercising its control over the citizenry, does not merely aid our ascent to greater heights of achievement, but also frustrates them, and "threaten[s] to overwhelm [and] to dominate" its residents.[24] Thus, the city simultaneously puts before us our aspirations in shining splendor—and indeed begins the process of fulfilling those aspirations—as well as warns us of the limits of such ambition with spectres of illness, madness, and violence.

The point at which the city transforms from being an aid to human ascendency to the agent of humanity's descent is the crucial turning point for this book's consideration of the undead. Standing above all the spectres mentioned at the end of the previous paragraph, the ultimate limitation the city forces us to face is that

21. Mumford, *The City in History*, 42.

22. Kasinitz, *Metropolis*, 3.

23. Cited in ibid., 108.

24. Ward, *Cities of God*, 30.

of human mortality, that great leveler of every lofty human ambition. At the same time that the infrastructure of the city facilitates the realization of human desires, Karsten Harries writes that the very same infrastructure functions as a signal of one's "temporal death-shadowed dwelling on earth."[25] Even as the city woos us as an Eden of fulfilled dreams and abundant lives, it also is a point at which citizens are made to grapple with the ending to those dreams through the ending of their very lives. In the city, we are made to wrestle with our own death, simultaneously resisting its approach while fearing its imminence. The city has become, to borrow from Bruno Latour, the site of "the same alternation between transcendence and immanence."[26] Put more accurately, it is the site of our alternation between immortality and death. To reiterate, the city serves as the convergence of Eden and heaven, making abundance converge with immortality, and in so doing it functions as the culminating point for a centuries-long project to perfect the human species and overcome what media historian Walter Kendrick has called the "modern fear of deadness."[27] Indeed, Kendrick notes a convergence also between the city and the horror that we behold in the portrayals of monsters in Gothic literature, and in other works designed to provoke horror from the eighteenth century onwards. Like the Graveyard Poets, the experience of horror embedded within the experience of the urban product of the book or the movie, was a calling to mind of one's mortality within the city. However, rather than welcomed as a reminder of the possibility of redemption, the forgetting of that possibility turned death into something to be resisted with life and limb.

The struggle with death within the city identified by theorists is played out in more concrete terms in the lives of its citizens. While the city suggests and warns, it is the citizens that embody and manifest the dreams and nightmares. As Pierre Bourdieu reminds us, the citizen is not merely an autonomous agent, but is

25. Harries, *The Ethical Function of Architecture*, 187.

26. Latour, *We Have Never Been Modern*, 34.

27. Morehead, "Zombie Walks, Zombie Jesus, and the Eschatology of Postmodern Flesh," 109.

primed to act in relation to his or her social—in this case, urban—surroundings. To borrow Bourdieu's words, the city works on citizens as a "community of dispositions"[28] that "acts within [citizens] . . . as the organizing principle of their actions."[29] Citizens within a city thus do not merely constitute a mass of individual residents. In the words of Cornelius Castoriadis, they are "walking and talking fragments of a given society . . . embody[ing] . . . the essential core of the institutions and significations of their society."[30] Given the city's implication of its residents in its extension and maintenance, it is necessary to consider how cities embody simultaneously the dreams of immortality as well as the boundaries of those dreams. The consideration of the citizen at this point must begin with the question: if the city is one that seeks godliness without God, how do citizens concretize this aspiration, and how does the zombie figure into this equation?

Before beginning to answer this question, recall that the postmodern city acts as the locus of a battle against mortality, where a city without God presses onwards to states of a Godless godliness. The sign of this supernatural state, Ward suggests, is a supernatural figure that has in the last two decades at least saturated the cultural imagination of postmodernity, the figure of the angel. "Our cultural horizons," says Ward, is one "crowding with hosts of angels"[31] as Western cultures become more "re-enchanted" and, augmented by the dazzling capacities of information technology, "produces dreams of transcendence."[32] This wording is suggestive, for Ward does not merely refer to the host of angel-themed product lines in clothing, television programs, books, and New-Age paraphernalia. He refers also to the *consumers* of these products.

As the city perfects the techniques of assuring its own immortality, its citizens, in living out their individual lives, are simultaneously "manufacturing and [being] manufactured by a

28. Bourdieu, *Outline of a Theory of Practice*, 35
29. Ibid., 18.
30. Castoriadis, "Radical Imagination," 332.
31. Ward, *Cities of God*, 206.
32. Ibid., 207.

contemporary angelology" where each strives to attain his or her own state of godliness by becoming an angel. The primary means of becoming an angel is going beyond the confines of our material and bodily existence, since the body, now under the spell of computerized augmentations, is treated as a "prison for angelic souls."[33] A way this plays out in practice can be gleaned from looking at Freudian psychoanalysis. Ola Sigurdson has in an article drawn our attention to the Slovenian philosopher Slavoj Žižek, who in turn drew heavily on the psychoanalysis of Jacques Lacan.[34] In that article, Sigurdson reminds us how Žižek regarded the human person as more than mere biology. Žižek draws upon Lacan's idea that psychic life involves an ineffable excess, an "essential object which is not an object any longer, but this something faced with which all words cease and all categories fail."[35] Every person, Žižek then argues, lives with an "excess of life," which drives him or her to tap into this "essential object" that exceeds the limitations of biological life and realize his or her status as an "infinite creature." This drive to become an "infinite creature" has parallels to the urban angel in more ways than one. There is, of course, the obvious drive to transcend biological life, but there is another, subtler, similarity. The psychoanalytic drive to live out an "excess of life" is, like the urban angel, not tapping into a transcendent horizon lying beyond one's immanence, but accessing that infinity *within* immanence.[36] Recall that, in the city, we are trying to be gods without God. Also, to flag what is to come, it is interesting to note that traditional Freudian psychoanalysis has called this urge to move beyond our biological life a "death drive," with Žižek using the label of "undeadness."

It will be necessary to return to Žižek's point of "undeadness" at a later stage. For now, note that this drive to become an angel by transcending biology, but still locking it within immanence, is brought about by two paralleling sociological processes, both of which are undergirded by advancements in manufacturing

33. Ibid.
34. Sigurdson, "Death Drive," 361–80.
35. Lacan, *The Ego in Freud's Theory*, 164.
36. Sigurdson, "Death Drive," 366.

provided for by the postmodern city. The first of these is the process of technological augmentation of one's body as a means to overcome the limits of the biological body, a process Ward describes as the production of "hybrids." In order to act on the drive to transcend without God, the embodied person needs to be enhanced. Parts of the person need to be enhanced to super-human—literally, over-the-human—levels. This urge to surpass the limitations of the human in order to attain transcendence and immortality has been circulating through our cultural imagination via depictions of human-amalgams, of hybrids—be they amalgams of human with machine or with some other animal or a supernatural entity. We find early examples of these hybrids in Gothic figures like Dr. Jekyll and Mr. Hyde and more contemporary alternatives in the mutants of *X-Men* comics and Neo in the Wachowskis' *Matrix* movie trilogy. What is important is that these hybrids are not seen as completely foreign objects locked in the confines of a page or screen. Instead, they have become integrated into the social fabric in which humans reside. In Ward's words, "we are all recognized to be hybrids now, for the natural order has buckled and warped" as more of our social and cultural life comes under a blanket of technological enhancement.[37] This is not so surprising in light of our existing modes of hybridization, from the mundane—such as the use of cars, pharmaceuticals, smartphones, and engineered food—to even the enhancement of bodies by cosmetics, hair extensions, eyelashes, tattoos, piercings, implants, and even artificial genitals. All of these are made available to anyone with the money to spend on them in malls, parlors, and boutiques in every major city, at least in the West, but also in parts of the developing world as well. In some cases, as in the case of engineered food, these hybrids are made available without the need even of the consumer's consent. So integrated into daily life have hybrids become that in most cases, they are not objects of revulsion, but of attraction and even seduction. Such capacities of hybrids to attract were already alluded to in Gothic figures like the undead Count Dracula. This trend towards the normalization

37. Ward, *Cities of God*, 210.

and even valorization of the hybrid finds its more contemporary expression, Ward says, in our valorization of cinematic heroes like Neo. Despite the differing types of hybrids, what binds them together is that, beneath the horror or thrall upon viewing such hybrids, lies an implicit desire to acquire the hybrids' attributes.[38]

While the cinematic trope of the hybrid articulates the desire to become angels in postmodernity, a second sociological trope articulates the fulfillment of that desire. The literary desire to mimic the technologically enhanced hybridity taking place on the page and the screen is being met by another technologically driven enhancement taking place on the human body. It is what Hervé Juvin labels the emergence of a new, technologically enhanced body in postmodernity. It is a body that is acting out the drive to overcome biological limitations, especially death, through the consumption of a slew of technological enhancements. The body in postmodernity is not only pushing the boundaries of capabilities or appearance, it is also pushing the boundaries of mortality—Juvin notes that in the last 100 years, we have tripled the average adult lifespan.[39] This is because the body as we know it has been increasingly augmented with the tools of modern medicine, supplemented by an array of anti-aging creams and other products, sales of which have accelerated in recent years.[40] Via the enhancements of medical science, infinity is being clawed back into immanence via the project "to extract time itself from the human body and give it immortality."[41] The production of this new hybrid body, growing less mortal by the day, is at once the production of the postmodern angel and the realization of the Freudian psychoanalytic drive to become that "infinite creature."

There is, however, more to immortality than fighting the signs of aging. As lifespans increase, what is also gradually emerging with this transcending of biological limits is an immortality

38. Ibid.

39. Juvin, *The Coming of the Body*, 4.

40. Juvin notes that in the four years leading to the publication of *The Coming of the Body* in 2010, sales of anti-aging products doubled. See ibid., 62.

41. Ibid.

defined as infinite possibility, even to the point of transcending the human form. With further augmentation, Juvin notes that the human body is no longer a pre-determined body, that is, one locked within the confines of tradition, culture, religion, blood-ties, or clan-affiliations. With technological enhancement and the overcoming of limit come greater diversity and the multiplication of available choices. The body, attached to these technologies, also undergoes a multiplication of possibilities in what that body would be and do.[42] The body need not be confined to a particular role, status, or even identity, with computer-generated models and technologically advanced surgical procedures able to mold flesh into all manner of forms and ideals. With a stroke of a scalpel, one can modify one's sex or race. The advancements and lowering of costs in tattooing has led to a proliferation of tattoo parlors beyond major urban centres to the neighborhood and the shopping mall, and with that the proliferation of possibilities of what the body can express. The decision to invoke the seeming magic of a mythical figure on one's body can be as easily made as the decision to get a cappuccino. Through the use of surgical technologies, one need not even want to look human anymore, with cases being reported of individuals using plastic surgeries to meld onto their person the visage of a reptile (as is the case of Eric Sprague, known more commonly as "The Lizardman") or a comic book character like the Red Skull. More subtly, it is interesting how, with the machinations of finance and life-insurance products, it is now possible convert one's body into a store of money, thereby furthering the body's horizons of possibility by converting the naked limitedness of the body to the naked possibility manifested in the sheer liquidity money.[43]

Even if one does not go to these extreme modifications of the body, the cultural pressure to produce the angelic body is still being operationalized in more banal ways, through diets, commercial gyms, and eating plans, which are proliferating at increasing speeds. A person can now find a dieting plan on a supermarket shelf right by the produce aisle, an aid in replicating the glistening,

42. Ibid., 11.

43. On this see Goodchild, *Theology of Money*, 31.

hard, fat-free, and virile bodies we see on the television and movie screen. If that were not enough, these angelic bodies can be enhanced even further in the malls, where the immortality *in* the muscles and skin can be supplemented by an immortality *upon* the muscles and skin. In the malls, one sees immortalities being marketed through the encouraging of shoppers to augment onto themselves the lives of the rich and famous through the acquisition of perfumes, clothing, homewares, accessories, or cosmetics used and owned by these angelic figures. In so putting on themselves the symbols of the rich and famous, the consumer is led to hope that the widened vistas of potential embodied by the lives of these icons could be made his or her own.

It might become apparent that both these drives—for immortality (defined as perpetuity and increased possibility) and for augmentation—converge in the act of consumption of a commodity. Also, Juvin reminds us, the kind of augmented immortality described above is a privilege attainable only by those with the money to pay for those commodities. This tying of immortality with one's ability to consume is the culmination of what Zygmunt Bauman has regarded as the transformation of societies from communities of production to a network of individual consumers. In Bauman's words, our social and cultural horizons have shifted and now "individuals are engaged . . . first and foremost as consumers rather than producers . . . . [There is] the substitution of consumer freedom for work." Most significantly, says Bauman, we have under such conditions come to see that "reality . . . is the pursuit of pleasure,"[44] and pleasure is to be found in the act of consumption. The legitimation of this change from the imperative towards production to that of consumption comes, not merely from freedom as "the choice between greater and lesser satisfactions."[45] It comes from the extending of Herbert Marcuse's observation that the satisfaction gained from consuming commodities has now transcended that of material needs to the "metaphysical."[46] Mar-

44. Bauman, *Intimations of Postmodernity*, 49.

45. Ibid.

46. Marcuse, *One Dimensional Man*, 8, 11.

cuse alerts us to the notion that there is now a new purpose for consumption. It is not merely to satisfy physical hunger, or merely obscure physical nakedness. The augmentation of the consumer's body via the acquisition and use of the commodity has now become the turning point whereby the consumer can, to borrow from Loudermilk, replace God in the role of the creator.[47]

It is precisely at the consumption of the commodity and the concomitant production of the postmodern angel, that the resident of a city enacts the city's "quest for life everlasting."[48] The godless heaven of the postmodern city is a shopper's paradise brimming with youth. We are awash with symbols of specifically this kind of heaven, a heaven whereby one is forever young and forever clasping an accessory of some description—think of the advertisements for youth culture, or the virile sleek executive types plastering our walls, street lights, billboards, and even toilets. The commodities we buy are now instantiations of eternal life, little sacraments that bring us to a secular vision of a new and everlasting life. It is the body itself, Juvin declares, that is the quintessential manifestation of this new immortal life—Juvin interestingly actually calls the body a "sacrament."[49] The postmodern cities we inhabit are now striving towards a heaven without the Beatific Vision, as residents try to create a whole plethora of beatific visions here on earth, enacting what Linda Badley calls a transcendence "of the body and through the body."[50]

Necrophilia

However, as the city and its citizens strive towards a godless heaven, hell lurks not too far behind. Recall Ward's point that as the city puts forward its aspirations to immortality, what follows closely behind it is an ominous disruption to those aspirations. Beneath

---

47. Loudermilk, "Eating 'Dawn,'" 96.
48. Ward, *Cities of God*, 44.
49. Juvin, *The Coming of the Body*, 94.
50. Badley, *Film, Horror and the Body Fantastic*, 7.

the seeming permanence of the sheen of the advertisement that says, "Be Forever Young"—there is a boutique that has branded all its apparel with its label "Forever New"—beneath the image of eternal youth, something threatens to expose the ephemerality of those representations and the goods that manifest them. Consumers might have noticed, at the close of the twentieth century, the irony at work wherein the desire for immanent immortality came at the time when the shelf-life of the goods we consumed was getting shorter and shorter. Hegelians might consider this a dialectic, coming to a synthesis in an immortality through constant consumption. Imagine two parallel thought streams being rained down upon the consumer. The first goes, "Consume, because this is not going to be around for long!" and the second goes, "Consume, because once you do, you will be around forever!" However, as one synthesis emerged at the close of the twentieth century, so another dialectic has appeared at the dawn of the twenty-first, only this time, it is a dialectic where the immortalized body, the angelic body, meets its opposite, namely the dead body. The paradox to note here is that, the more we try to make our bodies angelic, the more our bodies die. Whether we intentionally do it or not we are, bodies and all, moving towards an age of necrophilia.

This deadening of bodies is occurring first at the level of the social body as instantiated in the city. As the city strives to unseat God and proclaim a secular version of eternal life, it will inadvertently prepare itself for its death. There are several layers in which this kind of preparation for death is occurring. In *After Writing*, Catherine Pickstock draws our attention to the metaphysical bases of necrophilia. She sets the stage by claiming in no uncertain terms that "lurking beneath the surface of necrophobia is a much more fundamental necrophilia."[51] A way in understanding how this is the case lies not so much in the *fact* of a society's pursuit of immortality, but in understanding the *mode* by which that immortality is sought. Pickstock describes this pursuit not as an attempt to *banish* death, which is the way one might normally conceive of immortality. Instead, what our culture is trying to do is to *quarantine* death.

51. Pickstock, *After Writing*, 103.

In her words, modern and postmodern culture is an attempt to "prise death and life apart in order to preserve life [in the city] immune from death in pure sterility." The city is a sterilized laboratory, with the pursuit of immortality and its concomitant production of angels being more precisely a project in "seeking *only* life," in the form of what Pickstock calls a "pseudo-eternal permanence."[52] The urban landscape Pickstock points to is one with a zone of "pure life" on the one hand, and another zone of death on the other. However, Pickstock observes that in seeking eternal life by "removing all traces of death," what ends up happening is that there is an ironic surrender of life over to death such that those in the city find that "life has vanished with [death]."[53] The postmodern city thus manifests a metaphysics whereby a love of life is constantly giving way to a love of death, namely a "necrophilia." Eternal life is lived out as a constant vigilance against death, and the focus shifts to an obsessive lookout for the signs of death.

Having identified the signs of death, the city as laboratory is then dedicated to constantly taking death away from life, reifying life to an eternal category. The city is then a messianic bearer of eternity, whereby life on earth is made to bear the eternity of heaven. The trouble, however, is that eternity is a cross that life on earth cannot bear. This is because the burden of eternity is dependent on an openness to the transcendent and, in the modern quest for a heaven without God, the transcendent is the very thing that is also quarantined from life on earth. When life, now closed off from the transcendent, is expected to bear the weight of eternity that only the transcendent can bear, life will collapse under the weight of those expectations. Ultimately, not only is eternity lost; life itself is crushed under that cross of eternity, and dies with it. In piling on the burden of infinity onto a reified and finite life, life gets smothered and dies. Pickstock puts it differently, arguing that the reification of life encloses life into a self-contained unit, denying an openness that is required for life to be maintained. This metaphysics is manifested in the circulation of commodities—self-enclosed

52. Ibid., 104.
53. Ibid.

units of materials—as carriers of this kind of self-contained life bearing an eternity of aspirations. For Pickstock, the creation of life as an enclosed and manageable entity leads to the snuffing out of life. In spite of the differences in metaphor, the results are the same, for "in removing all traces of death," one only finds that "life has vanished with it."[54]

Put this way, one might notice that the urge to preserve finite life for infinitude sets the city up as a parody of the biblical narrative of the passage from temporal life on earth to the eternal life of the new heaven and new earth. This biblical element will be explored in greater detail in a later chapter. For now, one can see that the postmodern city is adapting the logic of an old Latin proverb: "If you want peace, prepare for war." The city has come up with its own metaphysical version that says, "If you want life, prepare for death." In setting itself up as the place where one ensures eternal life by being on the constant lookout for death, the city must ironically adopt a posture of "being-towards-death." Life in the immanently eternal city is thus a life of preparing itself to adopt what Ward calls a "Nietzschean embrace of death,"[55] or the courage to submit oneself unto death in an almost-Christlike fashion. One can only say "almost-Christlike" because in contradistinction to Christ, where the Son's life is marked by a constant openness to the transcendent Father, the city's explicit project is to embrace eternity *without a transcendent horizon*, without a reliance on turning to God. More importantly, precisely because there is no transcendence and no God to turn to, it would, John Dunne noted, "be more reasonable simply to recognize that if he must someday die there is nothing he can do that will satisfy his desire to live."[56] The paradox identified by both Pickstock and Ward is that an immanent eternal life must not only prepare itself for death, but also prepare itself for a life that has no further horizon than death. This vision of immortality that collapses the eternal transcendent into the contingent immanent is one that will eventually "conclude with the sovereignty of

54. Ibid.

55. Ward, *Cities of God*, 55–56.

56. Dunne, *City of the Gods*, 226.

death." With that vision the city as the fount of eternal life becomes "fundamentally a mausoleum,"[57] "offering a life which lives only by the production of death."[58]

As the social body dies, so too must the bodies of its constituents. As the eternal city on earth dies, so do the angels that are produced by its dazzling array of technologies and product lines. Indeed, Pickstock's use of the phrase "production of death" implicates an ironic harmony between the technological advancements the city deploys to produce postmodern angels and the death that is eventually dealt out. This scientific "production of death" segues into our consideration of zombies because, as Paffenroth notes, zombies "strain against the scientific framework that is imposed on them."[59] Recall that in the zombie it is a disease, a source of *death*, that is also its source of living well beyond the body's natural life-span. Furthermore, note that driving the zombie mythology is the understanding that medicine, that deposit of a scientific messianism, has not yielded any antidote to this condition. The zombie thereby mocks any scientific understanding of them. By extension, the zombie also mocks the scientific and technological underpinnings of postmodern attempts at angelology, by declaring with its own flesh death as the inevitable terminus of those attempts to endow flesh with immortality.

The zombie embodies this death at a number of levels. At a psychoanalytic level, Sigurdson suggests that such a death takes place the moment one acts upon the drive to transcend biological life and bring that "excess of life" Žižek spoke of and bottle it within the boundaries of sheer immanence—the production of the postmodern angel. It was mentioned earlier that Freudian psychoanalysis calls this drive to transcend biological life a "death drive." Following this Freudian line, Žižek labels this abundant remainder of life beyond its biological component with the word "undeadness."[60] Sigurdson's bringing both of these terms to our

57. Ward, *Cities of God*, 45.
58. Pickstock, *After Writing*, 105.
59. Paffenroth, "Apocalyptic," 147.
60. Sigurdson, "Death Drive," 366–67.

attention suggests that at a psychoanalytic level human life—or at least the kind of life that strives to attain infinity within sheer immanence—already comes with an inbuilt zombie.

This psychoanalytic zombification is enacted also at an anthropological level, in the death of the very flesh of these angelic citizens. The way to think of this death of the flesh is to begin with the drive to create what Juvin calls the "cult of the body beautiful." For Juvin, the body beautiful is more than an object mirroring life. The body beautiful is the "sacrament of life."[61] In the way similar to the Sacrament being the visible sign of invisible processes, the body in postmodernity stands as the visible sign of the angelic. To put it another way, the postmodern body is expected to contain within it the infinity that lies beyond the biological. More than a sign or a mere deposit in the instrumental sense, the body in postmodernity *is* the angelic, and thus *is* the exhaustive deposit of eternal life on earth. Juvin notes that this cult of the body is of a particular kind of body, a body that participates in and enacts Pickstock's city of eternity via the quarantining of death.

To understand the way the death of the body becomes quarantined, it is necessary to look briefly at *The Anticipatory Corpse*, by the philosopher and medical doctor, Jeffrey Bishop.[62] The central thesis to that book that is of relevance here is what Bishop identified as the baseline from which all knowledge in medical science is based, or what Bishop calls "epistemologically normative" for medical science. He interrogates the way in which medical science has limited its horizons to the realm of efficient causes. In other words, medical science is deliberately cut off from any consideration of ends that lead to flourishing, in particular the body's transcendent ends. Being focused solely on efficient causes, medical science is also deliberately cut off from primary causes. This may just sound like empty labeling, until one considers its relevance to the consideration of quarantining death. For Bishop, what this means in practice is that, in the name of staving off death, the most pertinent inquiries in medical science become the processes that

61. Juvin, *The Coming of the Body*, 94.
62. Bishop, *The Anticipatory Corpse*.

lead unto death, that is, the realm of efficient causes. What this means in practice is that the dead body is what sets the baseline for a medical science dedicated to the preservation of life. To use Bishop's words, "it is death . . . that motivates medicine."[63] The quarantining of death makes dead flesh the beginning and end of the investigative horizons of medical science. The array of product lines that then emit from the practices of medical science that we then see in popular culture—from pharmaceuticals to prosthetics, food, cosmetics, and even clothing—are thus similarly informed by the epistemological normativity of the dead body. Thus, the city and the postmodern angel are striving to embody immortality via a body is one constantly at war with the signs of aging. Indeed, Juvin says, the body in the postmodern city is given a moral imperative towards "banishing the very idea of aging, fatigue and wear."[64]

If the scientifically engineered constitutes the hallmarks of excellence, if that excellence is connected to the commitments of medical science to the epistemological normativity of dead bodies, and if such engineering is put into practice within the culture through the production of commodities that promote eternal youth, this means that paradoxically, *the promotion of eternal youth is grounded upon a foundation of a constant turning towards dead flesh*. Consumer lifestyles which link eternity with the consumption of products are fundamentally thus built upon a culture of death. The body in postmodern culture thus is a body that strives for eternity by eliminating the signs of time working on that body and is paradoxically a body that is continuously being delivered unto death.

This delivery of the body unto death is put into practice in the cult of the body beautiful through a flattened out vision of eternity in which eternity is located on the surface, where the immortal soul of the angelic citizen has been relocated to "the very surface of the skin."[65] Notice that the city that reifies life in the production of an angelic citizen, produces a particular kind of angelic citizen

63. Ibid., 15.
64. Juvin, *The Coming of the Body*, 94.
65. Ibid.

where appearance and visibility are the supreme moral impera-
tives. This should come as no surprise, since the postmodern city's
production of ceaseless warding off converges with what Foucault
identified as the emergence of a society being put under constant
surveillance.[66] For to fight the signs of aging is an enterprise in
highly focused technical management, and this management
requires all aspects of bodily life to be surveyed, quantified, and
rendered manipulable. Flesh becomes subject to metrics and constantly subject to the gaze of a scope or camera. In the process of
rendering every part of the body visible as a step towards producing
the postmodern angel, a kind of ocular-centrism sets in, such that
society becomes organized to privilege the seen, or more specifically "those subjected to the field of visibility, and who knows it."[67]
In such an ocular-centric society, "the new self is a visible self."[68] To
be an angel, it is imperative that one is *seen* to be an angel, and to be
seen to be an angel is to create a *visibly* angelic body. Little surprise
then that, when Ward speaks of the postmodern city as a city of
angels, such angels are produced through methods that glorify the
surface of the skin, where "angelic souls" collapse into "concepts
and construals of the perfect corporeality" via workouts, diets,
clothing, surgery, cosmetics, and most importantly, in photogra-
phy, video-imaging, and social media.[69] In short, the angel of the
eternal city in postmodernity is one whose contingent body bears
the cross of eternity by having its nude visage bare the soul on its
skin. More accurately, Juvin says, "the soul *is* the skin, as beauty, as
youth, as attractiveness."[70] This is a body that "gets what it wants,"
that is, a body completely subject to the direction of the individual

---

66. Foucault identifies the roots of this imperative to produce the surveillance society in the late eighteenth-century writings of Jeremy Bentham on the
"panopticon." See Foucault, *Discipline and Punish*, 195–230.

67. Ibid., 202.

68. Turner, *The Body and Society*, 171.

69. Ward, *Cities of God*, 207.

70. Juvin, *The Coming of the Body*, 102.

will. The body beautiful is the vehicle for "self-production, flanked by the demanding morality of physical beauty."[71]

However, as Pickstock noted, this striving towards eternal life compressed within the confines of the temporal ends up dissolving the temporal. It is no different with a body that tries to enfold the angelic into its skin. The consequences of translocating the angelic soul onto human skin are not lost on Juvin. Though he does not use the angelic language of Ward, Juvin's analysis of the body beautiful bears great resemblance to that of Ward's, especially in light of the former's observation of the body as the sacrament or bearer of eternal life. As will be shown, Juvin's observations about the fate of such a body bear a strikingly close resemblance to those of Pickstock's. As the body beautiful emerges, the body natural disappears.

To use Juvin's own words, "the advent of the body is also its disappearance," since the arrival of the body is also "accompanied by a growing phobia of its attributes, its nature, its physiology."[72] The body reified as the exhaustive wellspring of life itself ends up dissolving the actual body. This is because, for Juvin, the body that "gets what it wants" is a body that is on a "quest for indeterminacy." As mentioned earlier, the body as the vehicle for the autonomous individual will is also a body driven to "refusing to let age, gender or race have any bearing on the individual's professional, interpersonal, amorous, sporting or artistic capacities."[73] More than mere refusal, this drive to free the body from its ties to anything contingent, including ties to geography, community, bloodline, ethnicity, history, appearance, and even sex—Juvin at one point spoke of the "exemplarity of . . . transsexuals" in European media culture—is now "an article of the collective religion."[74] What this means, however, is that the actual body's attributes—its sweat, odors, wrinkles, hair, and hormones—precisely because they are contingent and obstacles to the limitless ambitions of the

71. Ibid., 95.
72. Ibid., 101.
73. Ibid., 61.
74. Ibid.

will, transform from being something natural to becoming objects of horror. Paradoxically, the quest for the angelic body in Ward's analysis culminates in a "horror of the flesh" in Juvin's,[75] a "growing phobia for its attributes, its nature, its physiology, a terror of the body's fleshly reality."[76]

It is at this moment where the angelic body starts to turn monstrous, it is here that flesh deadens and the once vibrant model gives way to the zombie. For in this angelic horror of the human flesh, human flesh is made to die. This is because construals of the flesh actually require more than biological tissue. They also require the connective tissue of community, language, and symbol, and what is occurring in the production of the angelic body is the stripping of those non-biological connections that give the flesh the very meaning that the "death drive" seeks to give that flesh. Reduced to sheer materiality or biology, the angelic body that "gets what it wants" meets up with a trauma as it realizes that it has no inbuilt vocabulary that articulates what it wants. The technologies that create the angelic body, for Ward, end up turning the body into an exhaustively material "clinical space" devoid of any meaning.[77] Thus, the more meaning is given to the immanent body, the more meaningless the body becomes. In short, the death drive turns the body to a piece of meat, made to be massaged, contorted, cut off, consumed, and killed off. A way to think this through is through the novel-cum-movie *American Psycho* as a demonstration of this mutation from the angelic to the monstrous. The novel's protagonist, Patrick Bateman, is seen by Ward as the "darkside of our fascination with the body."[78] Little wonder, seeing, as Laura Tanner noted, that if money is the god of Marx's capitalism, Bateman is the god of *American Psycho*.[79] More specifically, Bateman is the angel described in *Cities of God*. He is a person obsessed with bodies. He exercises and lotions his

75. Ibid., 101.
76. Ibid., 102.
77. Ward, *Discipleship*, 223.
78. Ibid., 224.
79. Tanner, *Intimate Violence*, 98.

own body to become that angel that the novel calls a "hardbody." The naked body portrayed in *American Psycho* is glorified beyond proper measure as the standard of truth and the real. At the same time, the body Bateman produces is a "billboard for the accumulation of brand names,"[80] only as good as the products that are placed on it or associated with it. It is a body that is worthy only to be used, both by himself and by others.[81] Bateman not only obsesses about his body, but is also obsessed about brand names, having no higher ambition than obtaining and consuming the slickest fashions, being at the trendiest restaurants, and sleeping with the most visibly beautiful women. Ward identifies the irony of this twofold obsession of naked bodies as truth, on the one hand, and the elevation of names over substance on the other.[82] The absurdity of this obsession is demonstrated at one point in the movie when Bateman swoons over a friend's business card, waxing lyrical about the texture of the stock card and the great significance attached to the font used to reproduce his name, address, and qualifications. He is not only besotted by the card, but finds in the card a measure of value that surpasses that of his own person. The perceived attack on his vanity then leads him to kill a homeless man in a rage. Ultimately for Bateman, the identities and the worth given to the bodies he interacts with, and even his own, slide seamlessly into the music, cosmetics, bottled water, and other products they in turn interact with. In Bateman's world bodies themselves, however angelic, have no independent significance or meaning.

Bateman thereby transitions from the angel to display zombie-like characteristics, and his lashing out on the material world becomes particularly acute when it comes to human flesh. When bodies become blank slates for brand names to hang on, he sees bodies as mere recipients of his vicious manipulations.

---

80. Ward, *Discipleship*, 224.

81. Ominously, Juvin says that an angelic body in our day is only "worth keeping alive so long as it brings satisfaction to itself and others." See Juvin, *The Coming of the Body*, 102.

82. Ward, *Discipleship*, 223.

In producing a "hardbody" and dissolving its meaning, Bateman has also dissolved the social body and produced only a poor copy. For Bateman, the angel is a man with no friends. His friends are a simulation of community, forums for displays of narcissism via the knowledge of products or fashions. What friends he does have he kills, he also kills strangers and, in parts of the movie, eats them. Who he does not kill or consume, he uses or manipulates to his own ends, including his fiance. In the end, Bateman's obsession with materials and his reduction of persons to mere tissue tears him from the connective tissue of real community beyond the mirages that he sleeps or cruises the bars and restaurants with. This is encapsulated in a paragraph where Bateman says of his life "where there was . . . life and water, I saw a desert landscape that was unending . . . so devoid of reason and light and spirit that the mind could not grasp it."[83]

Where *American Psycho* leaves off, a more recent literary and cinematic phenomenon, *50 Shades of Grey*, takes up and continues. In *50 Shades* we find another version of the postmodern angel, the multi-millionaire Christian Grey. Grey does not obsess over his body (though his physique is sufficiently attractive for the novel's female protagonist, Anastasia Steele), nor does he narcissistically clamor for fashions. What is accentuated in this angel, however, is the endless possibility brought about by immense wealth. In spite of these differences in angelology, the flesh of these angels take a similarly dark turn in treating flesh as meaningless recipients of manipulation. However, while Bateman does little more than emotionally manipulate his fiance, Grey is not hesitant to subject the bodies he supposedly loves to the same process of objectification and violence that Bateman only reserves for his supposed enemies. The "hardbody" here is Anastasia, the object of Grey's attention, who is similarly given an angelic visage, especially in the film adaptation of the novel. Her physique is slim and sensuous, her skin smooth, porcelainesque, and without blemish. This seeming embodied transcendence described by Juvin is given a brief homage in the trailer, in a moment where she almost glides

83. Ibid., 224.

on the floor. Her almost-childlike naiveté gives Anastasia a cherubic quality one finds in popular culture, that child angel found in cheap statuary and greeting cards on newsstands. Indeed, that parallel between Anastasia's angelic qualities and those on the pop-culture child angel becomes a subtle premonition of the fate of the angelic body as a commodified body. A sign to come is the showering of gifts by Grey onto Anastasia, and the culmination of the commodification of her own body is the famous subjection of her body to the acts of bondage and sadism that Grey metes out on her in the name of love. In a demonstration of the "death drive" referred to above, Anastasia willingly compromises the integrity of her flesh under a barrage of whippings. The love expressed is itself commodified, the result of an explicit contract replete with terms and conditions, including a non-disclosure clause which separates her from her friends. Thus, in spite of differences in plot, the endpoint of the body in each of these stories is the same, whereby bodies that seem to defy nature are made meaningless chunks of meat to be carved out, spanked, decorated by commodities and ultimately, left fundamentally alone.

While the events within these movies may be an extreme depiction, the extremity merely accentuates that crucial turning point at which angelic flesh becomes dead and zombie-like. In a critique of *American Psycho,* Laura Tanner drew a link between the dehumanizing processes of capitalism identified by Marx with the dehumanizing violence of Bateman as the epitome of a society made to consume materials. It is a society that is as vicious as it is shallow, and is often unleashing a vicious streak upon that very same materiality that it champions. Ward sees in this novel how a body that becomes the recipient of such attention will end up becoming a body "waiting to be controlled, coerced, and manipulated."[84] Tanner is more pointed. Citing Norman Mailer, Tanner noted the progress by which a society that makes money and "becomes altogether obsessed with the surface of things," enters "a period of absolute manipulation of humans by humans," with the "objective

84. Ibid., 222.

correlative of total manipulation [being] coldrock murder."[85] We see milder versions of this viciousness on flesh in the industries dedicated to the production of beauty, where the angelic "horror of flesh" translates into a model of beauty that many actual bodies cannot live up to, which makes these bodies only worthy to be manipulated by the artificially generated and disseminated images of beauty that it sees. They are also manipulated by the hands of the plastic surgeon who often, under the guise of expertise, singles out the body's non-angelic aspects and cuts away that non-angelic flesh to be replaced by seemingly beautiful artificial substitutes, be they noses, skin, cheeks, or breasts.

What the above ultimately seeks to bring into clearer relief is that, as the body becomes more angelic, it also develops a morbid fascination for dead bodies. The quest for the angelic body in the postmodern city is a quest that kills actual bodies, be those bodies biological or social. Not only does the postmodern angel become a killer, it also becomes a consumer of bodies, as the body becomes yet another commodity to be consumed and thrown away. Little surprise then that a city dedicated to the industrial production of the angel is also the city that sustains two other industries, pornography and prostitution. In pornography, bodies are commodified to their fullest extent. The bodies of porn stars are not bodies with meaning. They are shiny objects that fulfill not even desires, but drives and urges. Their flesh is consumed by the viewer, then cast aside for the next act of consumption. A less simulated corollary to that is the growing trade in prostitution. But in spite of the seedy underbelly associated with these industries, the kinds of bodies such industries presuppose blurs the distinction between these seemingly "exotic" industries and the more banal and mainstream industrial producers of consumer goods. There, bodies may not be consumed for titillation, but our desire for cheap goods similarly renders these bodies as meaningless objects of manipulation, limitless units of labor. The desire for bodies to act upon the "death drive" in the postmodern city makes these bodies undergo a "death drive" of their own as these bodies man the sweatshops and

85. Tanner, *Intimate Violence*, 97–98.

are squeezed for every last drop of labor to be put into our endless appetite for and infinite supply of ever cheaper shirts, electronics, furniture, and accessories. These products are tied to the bodies of those killed in war zones in mineral-rich countries that eventually find their way onto our batteries and conductors, of residents who live over deposits of oil, nickel, gold, and other materials and subsequently get displaced, of those who become dragooned into battles for control of those materials or get caught in the crossfire. Directly or indirectly all of us, even when we do not intend to, end up finding our life in becoming consumers of goods derived from dead flesh.

Conclusion

It is very easy to deem oneself too far removed from the fantasy of George Romero's movies to take seriously the notion that the zombies on screen are the mirror image of those watching the screen. However, that very fantasy may be serving as a useful mechanism with which a person may excuse him- or herself from the critique intended by Romero. However, seen in the light of the motif of the postmodern city's production of the angel in the works of Ward, Loudermilk, and Juvin, the efficacy of the fantasy as a shield begins to wear thin. The zombie's rotting flesh and drive to consume flesh, whilst not literal, is nonetheless allegorical. It is not a huge leap between the frenzy of the twisted flesh of the zombie and the shimmering elegance of the physique of Bateman or Grey, nor is the divide between the worlds of Bateman or Grey and ours a substantial one. We wear what Bateman wears, we are a society that produces "hardbodies," and we are a society that champions the wealth of Grey. Already, we are seeing societies like ours acting upon a postmodern version of the death drive, whereby finite flesh is made to bear the full force of the infinite, and subsequently turns from a thing of adulation to a thing of fear or reduced to a mere plaything. The slide of the angelic flesh of the body beautiful to the meaningless flesh of the zombie thereby seems inevitable.

While social theory has proven highly useful in bridging the gap between the reader and the zombie, the question remains as to whether the slide into the gaping maw of the zombie is unstoppable. To answer this, it is necessary to also ask the question as to whether social theory is our only fruitful standpoint to consider the zombie. The next chapter will consider how the theological standpoint can not only supplement the analysis of social theory with unique fruit of its own, but also bear the resources for reversing this slide into necrophilia.

3

The Zombie Is Jesus

Introduction

HAVING LOOKED AT OUR fraught cultural relationship with the zombie as the sharp end of a necrophilic culture, the question one must ask is, how should one evaluate this relationship? More specifically, how should a Christian evaluate this relationship? Moreover, does the Christian have anything unique to say about this relationship? In what follows, the assertion will be made that not only is the zombie a social statement, for the immortal-yet-rotting flesh and the frenzied desire for living flesh are also dripping with theological significance. As such, only a theological vocabulary would be able to decipher and critically engage the logic of the zombie.

This engagement will come at two levels. From a theological standpoint, this chapter will firstly critique the zombie as a subversion of theological vocabulary. At the same time, however, this chapter will also, from a theological standpoint, reconsider the degree to which the zombie is the inevitable and depressing cultural endpoint. It is necessary to start thinking about the zombie as a Christian because the zombie is not just a sad symbol of the futility of postmodern culture. It is also necessary because, in spite of this futility, the zombie nonetheless retains a powerful allure, an allure exemplified by the growing popularity of zombie walks. This allure is more than a fleeting fascination with a passing fad. Indeed, Linda Badley's point from the previous chapter concerning the attempt to achieve transcendence of and through the body, suggests that the fascination with the undead—zombies in particular—is charged with theological significance.

Documentation of the beginnings of the "zombie walk" are scarce, though the book *40 Years of Gen Con*[1]—"Gen Con" being a North American tabletop game convention—records the alleged first instance of a zombie walk in 2000 as an interruption to a vampire-themed event at the convention. Subsequent events explicitly billed as "Zombie Walks" began emerging in Canada in 2003 and has since spread around the *world*, with recorded events in cities such as Dublin, Mexico City, Nottingham, Sacramento, Santiago, and Sydney. Estimates of participation rates for such events range from small flash-mob style occurrences of seven participants to annual parades of 25,000 (as was the case in Buenos Aires in 2012). The zombie walk now enjoys its own category in the Guinness *Book of World Records*.

Despite the niche audience, the continuing popularity of the "zombie walk" suggests something more than the mere popularity of zombie-themed media. Indeed, the first chapter has already suggested that the interest in the undead is tapping into an otherworldly longing. John Morehead looks at the zombie walks not only as a new form of flashmob, but also an opportunity for participants to experience viscerally on their own person "transcendence through the body by adopting the imaginative identity of a living corpse." In the zombie, "death is transcended and the dead return to life,"[2] and participation in the zombie walk becomes an opportunity to experience this return from death to life. This "return to life" is suggestive of an explicitly theological structure operating within the zombie, a point that is not lost on Morehead. Indeed, Morehead seems to deliberately begin his analysis of zombies with reference to the "Zombie Jesus" motif and its deliberate

---

1. Laws, *40 Years of Gen Con.*
2. Morehead, "Zombie Walks," 109–10.

plays on scriptural references—as mentioned before, popularized allusions include Jesus' bodily resurrection from the dead and his injunction to his disciples to eat his flesh. It seems that the aim of Morehead is to point out that the zombie is not a vague homage to an abstract transcendent category, but a phenomenon that draws and plays upon the dense particularity of the Christian theological lexicon, such as death, resurrection, and the apocalypse.[3]

If Morehead is correct, then the cultural analysis in the previous section would provide us a good yet insufficient understanding of the public appreciation of the zombie phenomenon. Even as they refer to the transcendent, the analyses undertaken by social theorists remain vague in the absence of a theological vocabulary upon which the zombie phenomenon plays. It is with this in mind that consideration will be given to the zombie from the standpoint of Christian theology in the paragraphs that follow. It will be submitted here that this Christian theological standpoint must engage the zombie in a sacramental register, a point that even Morehead's work does not consider. It is asserted that looking at the zombie from the standpoint of sacramentality allows theology to not only look at the zombie conceptually. It also allows the church as the body of Christ, as an embodied phenomenon, to engage the corporeality of the zombie.

Christianity's God in the Zombie's Walk

Before going into the Eucharist, however, we need to look more generally at the way theology can help us make sense of the zombie. For the zombie, as we said, is a theological statement, but it makes a statement by being a parody of another, namely by being a parody of the "excess of life" that is found in Christ. In *On Belief*, Žižek provides an insight into the way Christ embodies the Freudian death drive, mentioned above. Recall that the death drive is the remainder within a person's life that transcends biological life, which Žižek at one point labels "undeadness." Referring to the

3. Ibid., 115.

Gospel of John, Žižek makes much of the verse in which Jesus says "I came so that you might have life, and have life to the full."[4] The "full" here is that remainder, that "undeadness" through which we transcend our biological life. Building on Žižek, Sigurdson looks at "Christ on the cross . . . as the incarnation of the excess" and our participation in Christ crucified as the point in which we "recognize this 'undead' dimension of ourselves."[5] There are echoes of Žižek's use of this motif in Pauline theology, whereby Paul makes reference to the distinction between two types of bodily existence. The first is *sarx* or the mere flesh that we inhabit on the one hand and the *soma*, a body that is animated and more importantly, redeemed by Christ, on the other. Though the parallel is not a neat one, it is interesting that Paul's *soma* is capable of an "excess of life" in a way similar to the psychoanalytic use of the term. This is indicated in Romans 8:11, where Paul reminds the church that the Spirit "who raised Christ from the dead, will also give life to your mortal bodies."[6] There is here an indicator that, in contradistinction to the negativity associated with earthly existence, Paul is pointing to redemption as a form of life *for* bodies, one that goes beyond the decaying flesh of *sarx* and is yet, in the body of Christ, nonetheless working within our own flesh.

The parallels between Paul's animated flesh (*soma*) and the psychoanalytic apprehension of the "excess of life" can sound crude if the passage to the Romans is all we have to rely on. However, this parallel can be put into clearer relief when one considers the distinction Paul makes concerning the ability—or lack thereof—to inhabit eternal life in the kingdom of God, which he makes in his first letter to the Corinthians. Paul makes it clear that "flesh and blood" (*sarx*) fundamentally cannot inherit the kingdom of God. The reason is made clear in Paul's next sentence, "nor does the perishable inherit the imperishable."[7] By contrast, *soma* is capable of entering into eternal life. In commenting upon Paul's use of *sarx*

---

4. John 10:10.

5. Sigurdson, "Death Drive," 368.

6. Rom 8:11.

7. 1 Cor 15:50.

and *soma*, James D. G. Dunn notes that it is the body—*soma*—that enjoys redemption, suggesting that redemption comes from the flesh being transformed into a body animated by the Spirit and in Christ.[8] For both Paul and Žižek, the lynchpin for this transformation or transcendence within the flesh is the person of Christ.

The parallels between Paul and Žižek end, however, at the point of identifying *when* this transformation takes place. The Pauline epistles make clear that this transformation comes at the moment of Christ's resurrection from the dead, since it is the Spirit who raised him from the dead. For Žižek, who does not take seriously the Gospel's claim of the resurrection, this ability to transcend the limitations of *sarx* and obtain this excess of life comes from Christ's passion, that dying to the world which is the point of convergence between human biological life and the death drive. For Žižek, the cross is where Christ taps into the "undeadness" and where that fullness or abundance of life—defined here as one's transcending of limitations imposed by circumstance—is actualized. Orthodox Christian theology will differ from Žižek on the significance placed on the cross, for Žižek dying to the world comes in the form of what he calls a "subjective destitution," through which one comes to accept the "horrible fact that any redemption is totally up to ourselves."[9] In other words, Christ's revolutionary act comes from the fact that the Son *gives up* on the Father's capacity to redeem and takes that responsibility upon himself. In orthodox Christianity, by contrast, Christ's revolutionary act comes exactly at the point in which the Son *surrenders* himself to the Father, a point encapsulated by the line in the Gospel "Father, into your hands, I commend my Spirit."[10]

As shall be demonstrated later, from the standpoint of Christian theology, Žižek is correct in identifying a historical and

8. Dunn, *The Theology of Paul the Apostle*, 71. Dunn alerts the reader to Paul's desire to affirm the Greek bias against "existence 'in the flesh'" at the same time as he wanted to affirm the Jewish assertion that bodily existence is necessary for a human existence. See 72.

9. Sigurdson, "Death Drive," 368.

10. Luke 23:46.

revolutionary significance to the passion, as well as identifying in Christ that dimension of "undeadness" in human desire. However, from the standpoint of Christian theology, Žižek is mistaken in locating Christ's radical act in the "subjective destitution" mentioned above, a move that is rooted in the rejection of the possibility of a bodily resurrection. For Christian theology, the fulfillment of the "death-drive" follows a quintessentially sacrificial logic and is not extinguished in Christ's act of surrender to the Father. Indeed, it is in his very surrender on the cross that Christ comes to embody the animated flesh of *soma*, that abundance in "undeadness," and it is the resurrection of dead flesh that vindicates that surrender. The post-resurrection narratives portray a flesh that cuts across spatial limitations, being able to escape recognition even when standing in full view, appear and disappear at will (as on the road to Emmaus), and pass through walls and locked doors. Ward also astutely observes that this *somatic* flesh even escapes the view of the reader of the Gospels, with the Gospels following Christ's every move until after the resurrection, whereby the body of Christ keeps "absenting" itself from the reader's gaze.[11] In other words, in his passion, death, and resurrection, Christ redeemed "undeadness" by inverting the notion of eternal life in dead flesh that we see in the zombie. "Undeadness" is not to be found in the pulling of transcendence into one's body. It is found in the act of surrender of that body to a transcendent God. The paradox here is that this surrender and the subsequent embrace of infinity is not a surrendering of the particularity of Christ's body. Indeed, such a surrender should be seen as giving greater emphasis on that very particularity. Considering the Eucharist might also draw the reader's attention to the importance of the particularity of Christ's body. By extension, this consideration should also aid in critically evaluating the kind of immortality the zombie offers, which is a kind that seeks the destruction of the particular.

11. Ward, *Cities of God*, 109.

Ecclesiology & the Body of Bodies

The Gathering, the Whole, and the Part

A way to think through the importance of the particularity of the body of Christ is to think of the zombie as embodying a kind of ecclesiology, one that parodies the ecclesiology within the body of Christ. The original Greek word, *ekklesia*, denoted not an institution primarily, since the institution was an outgrowing of a more fundamental act of gathering, one that is enacted at the level of the body, where the bodies collective form a corporate entity. Thus "ecclesiology," while primarily a theology of the church, can also be taken here to denote a theory whereby a body gathers other bodies as a locus of redemption.

Considering the zombie as embodying a kind of ecclesiology may not be as far fetched as it may first appear. An essay by Ashley Moyse considered how acts of gathering—in this case of the humans into traveling or sedentary communities in *The Walking Dead*—enacted a form of salvation, namely an economy of resistance against the zombies through acts of solidarity, which in turn enacted the virtue of hope.[12] This coupling of faith and belonging one finds on a television series finds echoes in the Scriptural accounts. Stanley Hauerwas noted that the Old Testament attests to the link between salvation on the one hand and a gathering of people on the other. It was in one's belonging to a distinct people, Hauerwas asserted, that one's salvation was enacted.[13] Avery Dulles argued similarly when speaking of faith as the starting point on one's path to salvation after Christ. Faith, Dulles argued, was grounded in one's decision to become a member of a gathered assembly, as "Christian faith has a divinely given content that can be known only through reliance on the community that already professes it."[14]

---

12. Moyse, "When All Is Lost, Gather 'Round."
13. See Hauerwas, "Citizens of Heaven."
14. Dulles, "The Ecclesial Dimension of Faith," 420.

Note, however, that salvation via gathering is not something that is unique to humans in the zombie genre. For zombies enact a salvation of their own, gaining their cultural potency as immortal beings by being a "wretched gathering where death embodied haunts."[15] Consider how, in pop-cultural construals of the zombie, it is at its most potent when attacks are undertaken in groups, overwhelming any resistance to its bite by sheer force of numbers. A lone zombie, by contrast, is relatively benign and is often easily dispatched, with the only exception being when they ambush a person. The same logic of potency by numbers applies even in the more sedate setting of the "zombie walk." As Paffenroth points out, part of the appeal of the zombie walk lies in the fact that otherwise ordinary individuals can express some modicum of potency in the flash mob, as it is in the context of the flash mob that the individual can obtain that visceral experience of immortality.[16] The mob is necessary to generate individual experiences, as Ward points out, since the singularity of one's experience is generated through a communication of knowledge via one body's connection to another. There is, in other words, a "transcorporeality" of knowledge, whereby notions of how a body experiences is "constituted in and through its relations with other bodies."[17] However, the transcorporeality of *this* particular flash mob—the zombie-walk—is that the transcorporeal operation is such that the relationship begins to obscure the particular persons that are in relation. To put it more practically, an individual's experience of immortality, or even potency, in the zombie walk is dependent on the disappearance of that particular individual zombie into a horde. For apart from slight variations, there is little to distinguish one zombie from another visually. To stand out in a zombie walk and emphasize individual identity, acts as a negation of the zombie motif. Thus, to be a zombie is to accept the death of the particular subject and its absorption into the anonymity of the horde.

15. Moyse, "When All Is Lost, Gather 'Round," 126.
16. Morehead, "Zombie Walks," 117.
17. Ward, *Christ and Culture*, 168.

As the zombies gather to walk, Christ too enacts a gathering of his own in the Eucharist and in his walk at the passion. Recall that, in the Gospel of John, the passion was indicated by Christ as the locus whereby he will "gather all things to [himself],"[18] with the locus of that gathering being his own body. At the Lord's Supper, Christ names the Eucharistic elements as "my body" and the site of the "new and eternal covenant," a covenant that is sealed with his walk to the Place of the Skull. This action of Eucharist and passion implicating the same body is rich in its implications for our bodies. What one sees at the first instance is that the body is not located in a specific site. It encompasses the species, the Garden in Gethsemane, the torture chambers and the cobblestones of Jerusalem, the Place of the Skull, the cross, and the tomb. Every minutiae of the earth—even the soil[19]—has become imprinted with the presence of Christ's body. In all these Christ's body is present.

If we set aside the lens of piety momentarily and merely observe the phenomena, one might notice a parallel to the zombie in one respect. There is a disappearance of particular identities into the many, enacted from the beginning by Christ's dispersal of his body to his disciples who, in obedience to him, took and ate his body. Christ is no longer a discernible and distinct entity, occupying only one place at a time. It would seem that, as in the case of the zombie horde, Christ's particularity has disappeared. However, there is an important distinction that sets the Eucharistic gathering apart from the gathering of zombies, into which particularities disappear and are obliterated. Graham Ward notes that part the problem with drawing too neat a parallel between the Eucharist and zombies lies in the fact that those who make such parallels too easily "take the human to be a measure of the Christic."[20] In other words, drawing too neat a parallel between Christ and the zombie

---

18. John 12:32.

19. This is demonstrated by the action of Christ's spitting on the ground, mixing his bodily fluid with the soil to create the healing paste for the blind man. The blind man is healed not because of the soil per se, but because of its making space for the body of Christ. See John 9:6.

20. Ward, *Cities of God*, 97.

ignores the fact that Christ's body in the Eucharistic species—and thus Christ Eucharistic body—bears within it a corporeal logic that is very different from the biological body and by extension a logic distinct from that of the zombie. Furthermore, it is the Eucharistic body of Christ that sets the tone for how the physical body of Christ is to operate as a mystical body during his passion. Indeed, as shall be demonstrated later, the Eucharistic body is what sets the measure not only of the Christic, but also the human.

In the Eucharistic body, one will find that it is the degree to which the body is displaced, broken, and consumed by others, that the body becomes Christic. However, this Eucharistic body is not the displaced body that disappears into the mass by being torn into pieces and being consumed by the zombie horde, never to be seen again. In the dispersal of the body of Jesus, Jesus does not lose his identity and disappear into the mass. Ward asserts that in the Eucharist, we see a compendium of the way the body of Christ "is represented in the Scriptures, and the tradition's reflections upon the Scriptures, as continually being displaced,"[21] and yet acts as the center of gravity around which other bodies gather. In other words, the body of Christ does not disperse in order to disappear. Rather, it disperses in order to displace, to stretch out into a net that catches all bodies into itself.

Before investigating how the displaced body gathers other bodies to itself, it is first necessary to investigate how the body of Christ retains its integrity in spite of its dispersal. To this, one must turn to the Eucharist and how its structure transforms the modern relationship between the one and the many. This relationship between the one and the many is demonstrated at the fraction of the Eucharist. At first glance, the act of breaking the Eucharistic body into pieces might seem to follow the zombie's logic of dissolving the one into the many. However, William Cavanaugh reminds us that a unity still persists within the fractioned Eucharist. It is a unity where, instead of the *breaking* up the whole into parts, the fraction *multiplies* the whole into the many parts. In other words, instead of the whole disappearing into a mass of parts, every part articulates

21. Ibid.

the whole that came before it. This unity amid the multiplication of wholes in the Eucharist, Cavanaugh argues, can be witnessed in terms of the simultaneous identification of the local church with the universal church. Each local Eucharistic altar acts as the site for the universal church, since each local Eucharist "makes present not the part of Christ but the whole Christ, and the eschatological unity of all in Christ."[22] We see this in the way that, in Eucharistic theology, every piece of the species that is distributed is not a case of giving a body, or arm or leg, of Christ, but the *entirety* of his body. In every particular Eucharistic altar around the world, there the entirety of Christ's body is made viscerally present. Thus, "in the Eucharist . . . a hidden way of being embodied is being manifest," one that refuses to allow the distinct identity of Christ to be lost even as it stretches out into the many places and people before, during, and after the Lord's Supper. Even as it fractures into the many, the "whole Body of Christ is present in each fraction of the elements."[23]

Liturgy, Consumption, and Life

The zombie as parody of Christian ecclesiology comes into clearer relief when one compares the logic of consumption set within the structure of the Eucharistic liturgy on the one hand and that of a zombie rampage on the other. In other words, zombie ecclesiology parodies the Christian not only as a mapping out of the body onto others, but also as a liturgy insofar as it is a work of the public (in Greek *leitourgia*). For the "Romero Zombie," the drive to consume flesh has become the defining trait of its immortal life, the center of gravity around which three other zombie-related tropes orbit. The first orbital trope concerns the way a zombie's drive to feed is a taking away of the biological life of the living, an incorporation of the living body of the victim into the dead body of the zombie, thereby ending the life of the living. The second orbital trope

---

22. Cavanaugh, *Theopolitical Imagination*, 50.

23. Ibid., 114.

concerns the way the zombie's "feeding" on the victim, whilst eras-
ing the life of the latter, does not lead to any concomitant increase
in the vitality of the former. The zombie can literally go for an
eternity without food, and what food it does consume does not
make the zombie any more alive, whether in terms of physical or
intellectual upbuild. In other words, the death of the victim does
not translate into life for the zombie. In an act of consumption by
the zombie, everything dies or remains dead, a fact put on graphic
display by the fact that the zombie does not eat the whole victim,
but only takes scraps and moves onto the next living person. This
rampant partial consumption generates a red carpet of death and
has the effect of laying death bare for other potential victims, and
for the viewer.[24] The third orbital trope is that any transformation
that does take place comes in the form of the living being transformed into the dead. The ecclesiology of the zombie, therefore, is
one where consumption of the living begets the exponential multiplication of dead consumers of flesh.

Seeing the zombie in a liturgical light shows the liturgy of the
zombie rampage to be a diametrical opposite of the structure of
the Eucharistic liturgy. The key in locating this juxtaposition is the
act of breaking and consumption of flesh. Though the phenomena
may look similar, the logic operating in each could not be more different. In the zombie rampage, flesh is treated in a possessive fashion, torn and consumed to satisfy a drive to take something else
for one's own. The victim is quite obviously an unwilling one. By
contrast, though there is a breaking and an act of consumption of
flesh in the Eucharist, this is preceded first by an act of willing surrender of that flesh by the victim, expressed by Jesus' exhortation
to his disciples at the Lord's Supper to "take and eat" his body. As
Alexander Schmemann has noted, the Eucharistic body's structure
of products for consumption, namely bread and wine, acknowl-
edges the consumptive aspect of food. At the same time however,
these elements participate in a liturgical act in which offering that
food to God in a sacrifice of praise forms the epicenter. The act
of offering is the epicenter because the liturgy's founder, namely

24. Paffenroth, "Apocalyptic," 147.

Christ, imprints that pattern in his exhortation of his disciples to take and eat his body at the Lord's Supper. Christ, having identified the Eucharistic food as his body, then willingly breaks it and gives it over to be consumed. This act of the victim willingly giving over himself to the other, argues Ward, is of "paramount" importance.[25] That Christ, the new prototype of man, posits a pattern of surrender in the act of consumption means that giving over oneself willingly to another is not an unnatural act. Indeed, Schmemann argues that the Eucharist unveils the degree to which we have taken what is unnatural—the act of possessive consumption—to be the norm in the human condition. In a diametric opposite to this normalization of possessive consumption the archetype of the human gives himself over to be consumed, from the Lord's supper up to his crucifixion, declaring to the world that it is the pattern of surrender that fulfills the human person. In Schmemann's words, the act of handing over fulfills the "Eucharistic function of man, his very fulfillment as man."[26]

This handing over by the new Adam and the archetype of man has rich implications for us as well. Christ's handing over is, at one level, a handover of his physical body to be crucified. But it is simultaneously a handing over of that body over to the Creator, an act already initiated in the Son's offering of the Eucharistic body to the Father at the Lord's Supper—the Synoptic Gospels mark the pattern of Christ taking bread, giving thanks, then breaking it to give to his disciples.[27] It is an act that continues on in his passion and culminates in the handing of his body to be crucified, and the subsequent entrusting of his spirit into the hands of the Father.[28] Handing over one's body into the hands of others is at complete cross purposes with a culture that posits the individual will and imagination as the source of all agency and creativity, with the body as a mere instrument of that will. The act of handing over and making one's body subject to the wills of others is an act of

25. Ward, *Cities of God*, 102.

26. Schmemann, *For the Life of the World*, 34.

27. Mark 14:22; Luke 22:19; Matt 26:26.

28. Luke 23:46.

recognition that the source of agency does not lie in the individual will. Agency reaches far beyond the individual will to someplace else, indeed to some*one* else. As Michel de Certeau once wrote, to be a subject in space and time—to be a body—is to unavoidably "be other and move towards the other."[29] To be a body is to be a subject where agency is grounded in reaching beyond the confines of the individual will and reaching out to another. Furthermore, Christ's act of handing over his body is not confined to a horizontal handing over to other wills. This horizontal dimension of surrender to others is also coupled with a vertical dimension of surrender to the Father. Thus, in Christ, we see that agency of an embodied subject is radically other in the sense that agency is grounded in openness to a transcendent other. It is a recognition that the source of agency in bringing out the immortal subject of psychoanalysis only comes from the other side of a transcendent horizon rather than within sheer immanence.[30]

Moreover, the logic of the Eucharist is one that requires more than mere openness to the God who transcends and creates all things. While de Certeau spoke about a *moving* towards another, Maurice Merleau-Ponty reminds his readers that to be an embodied subject is to go beyond mere motion. Merleau-Ponty spoke about a person's body being "intervolved" with his or her environment. To be an embodied subject, Merleau-Ponty says, is to be "inseparable from this particular body and this particular world,"[31] indicating a deep connection to the environment, and those within it. This deep connection suggests that as an embodied subject one is not only constantly moving towards another, but also constantly *committing* my body to the bodies of others, whether these bodies are physical, social, or environmental, making these bodies my own and allowing my body to be made their own. In Merleau-Ponty's words, existence is a "movement through which man . . . involves himself in a physical and social situation which then

---

29. de Certeau, *The Practice of Everyday Life*, 110.

30. Sigurdson, "Death Drive," 367.

31. Merleau-Ponty, *Phenomenology of Perception*, 431.

becomes his point of view on the world."[32] Or in stronger terms, to exist as an embodied subject is to affirm with Merleau-Ponty that "my body is made of the same flesh as the world."[33] Having opened oneself, and moved towards that transcendent other, it is also necessary to hand oneself over to God by committing oneself to God, in a genuine act of participation in the truly transcendent. This is in contrast to Žižek depiction of Christ, a Christ whose significance lies in his erasure of any human dependence on God. For Žižek, the crucifixion of Christ is highly important because it is an act of abandoning the God who abandoned him and is the point where "God loses the character of the transcendent Beyond and enable[s] direct communication between God and humanity . . . because there is no longer any transcendent God with whom to communicate."[34] This account of Christ crucified is diametrically opposed to the Christian tradition's account of that crucial event. Instead of abandonment defined as self-reliance, as Žižek would have it, the kind of abandonment the Christian tradition associates with Christ crucifixion is typified by a surrender of self to the transcendent Other. In the words of Hans Urs von Balthasar, "true abandonment means constantly giving back to God all that He has given us and 'returning it all to the ground and source whence it sprang.'"[35] In other words, the abandonment prescribed by the Christian tradition is a participation in the very transcendence that Žižek exhorts us to abandon.

Furthermore, this participation is complete when, as one reaches towards God, God pulls the one reaching towards Himself, enfolding into Christ the one reaching into the Godhead.[36] As one reaches towards and commits to God, and as the body is enfolded into Christ, the body is stretched to make way for God to abide in it, as the body of Christ in turn stretches and maps itself onto

32. Merleau-Ponty, *Sense and Non-Sense*, 72.

33. Merleau-Ponty, *The Visible and the Invisible*, 138, 248.

34. Žižek, *Did Somebody Say Totalitarianism?* 51.

35. von Balthasar, *Metaphysics in the Modern Age*, 54.

36. Ward, *Cities of God*, 124.

creation.[37] Note the Gospel of John where the life of the disciple is underpinned by Christ's command to "abide in me as I abide in you."[38] The idea of co-abiding between God and an embodied subject, Ward suggests, resists the easy separation of the embodied and the spiritual, whether in the Christian life in general or the work of redemption in particular. For Christ's resurrection is not a rejection of the Eucharistic embodiment that was celebrated at the Last Supper. Indeed, the Eucharist anchors the assurance that the resurrection "does not mean that he has rejected or abandoned embodiment," but now embraces a new embodiment that escapes physical limitation.[39] It is an embodiment that can be broken and yet multiply into living wholes. It is an embodiment where flesh consumes by being consumed by flesh. Indeed, it is precisely through being broken, multiplied, and consumed that the body of Christ comes to be extended. It is precisely this Eucharistic embodiment, which works within yet escapes the confines of embodiment, that makes possible the kind of stretching of the body mentioned above, and the co-abiding necessary to facilitate it. The Christian life therefore, when set against a Eucharistic backdrop, is one of mutual co-abiding between the *soma* of the transcendent-yet-immanent flesh of Christ and the *sarx* of our own merely immanent flesh. Human flesh gets the life of angels only insofar as it part-takes of what Aquinas in his *Sacris Solemnis* hymn called the "bread of angels"—the *panis angelicus*. Set in a Eucharistic key, the "death drive" can only be fulfilled if that drive for transcendence causes flesh to not only reach beyond itself, but also constantly to surrender itself to God and to others. This surrender leading into enfolding and then co-abiding unpacks Paul's urging the Christians of Rome to "offer your very bodies as a living sacrifice, holy and pleasing to God."[40]

In light of the Eucharistic structure canvassed above and its significance in relation to the zombie, Paul's exhortation above, the

37. Ward, *Christ and Culture*, 177.

38. John 15:4.

39. Ward, *Christ and Culture*, 177.

40. Rom 12:1.

exhortation to live as living corporeal sacrifices, becomes rich in meaning. There are parallels between the postmodern and Christian attempt to create angelic or holy bodies. Insofar as these bodies become worthy only of narcissistic adulation, however, they ultimately end in death and the disfigurement of the zombie. By contrast, the body oriented by the Eucharist is "holy" only insofar as it is "pleasing to God," insofar as it goes beyond itself and is pleasing to another, and a transcendent Other at that. There is attached to "holiness" a twofold condition. Holiness is dependent on alterity as opposed to the self-centered "holiness" of the postmodern angel, which is grounded in the adulation of the self by others. In the light of Christ's giving over of himself to the Father, holiness is also dependent on handing oneself over to transcendence and not the Freudian "death drive," which seeks to exhaustively pull transcendence into the static center of immanent flesh.

Another point of divergence emerges concerning where life goes at the moment of consumption of flesh. As opposed to the zombie's act of consumption, taking life away, the Eucharistic act of the giving over of Christ's body to be consumed *gives life* to the world. With the vertical dimension of handing over mentioned above, there is also a horizontal dimension, the structure of which can be gleaned in the account of Jesus' healing of the man with the "virulent skin disease," recorded in the first chapter of the Gospel of Mark.[41] Though a short passage, the sequence of actions taking place provide a key by which Christ's saving action *vis-à-vis* his creation through acts of handing over can be understood. It is also a highly informative passage in terms of our understanding of Christ's relationship with the zombie. We see at one level an obvious fleshly deadening, at the level of the skin. However, physical death is not the only form of death brought about by this disease since, according to Mosaic law, the man is also suffering a social death in terms of a severance from the social body.[42] There is thus a death of two bodies, the physical and the social. With

41. Mark 1: 40–45.

42. "He shall live alone, his dwelling will be outside the camp." See Lev 13:46.

these two simultaneous deaths comes the destruction of particular identity, as the distinctiveness of the citizen now gives way to the indistinctiveness of a diseased body which, according to the law of Moses, provides no further identifier than a covered lip and shouts of "unclean, unclean."[43] We see here the destruction of the identity of the man into a nameless and marginalized mass of disease and the destruction of a particular person into the horde of diseased bodies. The episode of the man's healing in the Gospel of Mark highlights the structure of Christ's willing surrender of his body to the other in the economy of salvation, as opposed to the possessive consumption of the body of the other by the zombie. For recall that the zombie is one that takes possession of others' flesh into itself. The zombie itself remains static and pulls flesh into itself, and the movement of the flesh of the living is not only passive, but results in an all encompassing death. In the structure of the Gospel's depiction of Jesus' saving act, on the other hand, the complete inverse is true. The sequence of Jesus' action begins with a response to a call of "if you want, you can cure me,"[44] the response being a reaching out and touching of the diseased corpus. It is at this point that the sequence of handing over begins, for under Mosaic Law, any touching of any diseased body incorporates the person doing the touching into the body of disease, into a corpus of death. Rather than remaining static, as it is in the case of the zombie, we see a dynamic exchange taking place between Jesus and the diseased man. Following the Eucharistic logic highlighted above, the man, cured of his fleshly death and restored to his community, is enfolded into the constantly extending body of Jesus by the former's being touched by the latter. In the process, the *sarx* of the once dead man now shares in the *soma* of the animated flesh of Christ, sharing in its new life. By contrast Jesus, though not stricken with the fleshly death of the man's disease, nonetheless assumes the social death the disease brings through the displacement of his body and mapping that onto the body of the previously sick man. This is indicated by his inability to move within the towns now that the

43. Lev 13:45.
44. Mark 1:40.

news of this cure has spread, and the Gospel passage almost concludes with the poignant line that Jesus "could only stay outside in the lonely places."[45] Be that as it may, this death is not the endpoint of the action of displacement of Christ's body. In the Gospel, the death of isolation of Jesus brought about by his displaced body is but a precursor to the generation of new life indicated by isolation's opposite, namely a gathering up. This gathering is hinted at in the Gospel passage when the isolation decisively concludes with the line "and yet people came to him from everywhere."[46]

A couple of salient themes emerge from this passage. In the first instance, Mark's account of this healing puts on visceral display the Eucharistic logic of the embodied life of Christ. Redemption is not a command from a static center but a dynamic and embodied process of displacing one body into another. In other words, an economy of redemption characterized by a Eucharistic logic of displacement comes in the form of the Savior's assuming the place of the one to be saved. This salvific action by Christ is one of handing over himself to assume every aspect of the human condition, up to and including death. Even sin and its fruits figure in this process of handing over, with Paul noting that God "made him who knew no sin [i.e., Christ] to become sin on our behalf."[47] Salvation as a

45. Mark 1:45.

46. Ibid.

47. 2 Cor 5:21. The passage does raise a question on whether Jesus takes on sin as part of his assuming the human condition, thereby making him a sinner like us. This seems to fly in the face of Heb 4:15, where the author to the Hebrews spoke of Christ being "like us in all things but sin." The reconciliation of how a person that knows no sin to become sin, however, seems to have been made with ancient authors like Cyril of Alexandria and John Chrysostom. Cyril writes that "We do no write that Christ *became a sinner* but being righteous, the Father made him a *victim for the sins of the world*" (Letters 41:10). Chrysostom similarly writes "God allowed His Son to suffer as if a condemned sinner, so that we might be delivered from the penalty of our sins" (Homily on 1 Corinthians 11:5). In other words, Jesus does not take on the human condition insofar as he becomes a sinner, but certainly takes on the *fruits* of that sin, which is death. See Bray and Oden, *1–2 Corinthians*, 252–53.

This may raise the question as to whether Jesus really took on the human condition fully. But as Steven Guthrie suggests, Jesus presents the archetype of humanity, thereby exposing the degree to which sin is actually an aberration

handing over means that Christ hands his animated body over to assume the condition of the fruit of sin, namely dead flesh. The economy of salvation can be described as one where Christ assumes the condition of the zombie as the undead embodiment of sin.

In the second instance, though Ward is correct in identifying this displacement as of paramount importance, it is also of paramount importance to remember that the salvific dimension of displacement is due to the refusal of the body by Christ to dissolve into another body. Even though Christ does indeed assume the condition of the zombie, it does not result in an ultimate disappearance of his living flesh into the flesh of the dead. Seen in the light of the Eucharist, the act of handing over one's body and the accompaniment of what seems like a dismembering of flesh, actually constitutes a multiplication of sites by which life can spring forth. We see a hint of this in the above Markan episode where the healed man, now enfolded into the body of Christ, tells of his cure by Christ[48] and becomes an extension of the life-giving process of gathering up into Christ. This can only be so when displacement is set against the backdrop of the Eucharist because, in the patristic understanding of the Eucharist, consumption of the Eucharistic body by the congregant is not an act of dissolving the body of Christ into the body of the congregant. While the life of *sarx* may function by this logic, the life of *soma* may operate only when the congregant becomes consumed by what is consumed, and the body of Christ is mapped onto the body of the believer in the act of Eucharistic displacement.[49] This dynamic is made explicit in Book VII of Augustine's *Confessions*, where he describes the Eucharist as "the food of the fully grown," where Christ says, via Augustine, "grow and you will feed on me. And you will not change me into yourself like the food your flesh eats, but you will be changed into me."[50] In this mapping out of the animated flesh of Christ onto the

---

of the human condition rather than a hallmark. See Guthrie, *Creator Spirit.*

48. Mark 1:45.

49. Cavanaugh, *Theopolitical Imagination*, 119–20.

50. Augustine, *Confessions*, 124.

flesh of the believer, we see also the absorption of dead flesh by the living, where "death is swallowed up in victory" by all bodies being incorporated into the body of Christ.[51]

It is at this point of the absorbing of *sarx* into *soma* that we see the Christianization—and thus the redemption—of the zombie. What was once a monstrous attempt at immortality by one via the possessive dismemberment of others, suddenly realizes its *telos* only in the light of a Eucharistic logic. The immortality sought in the "death drive" comes only from a handing over of the *sarx* of one's flesh to the *soma* of Christ's body in a Eucharistic co-abiding. Christ's redemption of flesh as a precondition of immortality comes not from our efforts to assume the condition of a god, but from God's work in assuming the condition of a slave, a slave for whom flesh needs to be consumed to sustain only a modicum of life. In other words, the redemption of flesh comes only when Christ assumes our condition of the zombie. Having assumed that condition, Christ then *reorients* the zombie by showing to it the true path to immortality, the true trajectory and end of the "death drive." The production of the postmodern angel and the need for Christ's redemption of flesh may be paths that begin with the death drive, but the differences between the path of the Romero-zombie and the path of Christ cannot be starker. While the death drive of the former spurs on a pattern of possessive behavior, that of the latter enjoins a pattern of surrender and sacrifice of self to another. While the former forges a path of forced displacement of other bodies for one's own, the latter mandates a displacement and handing over of one's body to others. While the former causes all that has life to die, the latter ends in the distribution of life.

The final way in which the Eucharist redeems the zombie is in the recalibration of the worldview against which the act of consumption takes place and finds its logic. This recalibration is from one in which all life hurtles inexorably towards the finality of death (as it is with the zombie), to one in which the inevitable end of all things is joy (as it is with the Eucharist). At first glance, the equivalence of death and joy to consumption might sound like

51. 1 Cor 15:54.

an odd one until one notices that, in a context saturated with the narratives relayed by advertising, consumption is tied with joy. This link between advertising, consumption, and joy will be developed on later. For the moment, consider how displays of zombies, amidst the flesh-eating and its resistance by survivors, are often done with a heaviness of heart or sense of foreboding. There is a sadness and anxiety to even the most comic portrayals and endings in cinematic portrayals of zombies. At best, there is either some uneasy truce made between zombies and humans (as is the case with *Shaun of the Dead*), or a semblance of stability is reached whereby the consumption of flesh by zombies is merely held at bay, with the anxious expectation that the rampage can repeat itself at any point in the future (as is the case with the *Resident Evil* series of movies). In both cases, each outcome is reached through gory displays of violence, and what seems like a happy situation still has the spectre of death looming over it.

Moreover there is, with varying degrees of subtlety, a denigration of anyone being too happy, displaying too much virtue, or being too gentle. Such displays of goodness are portrayed as obstacles to survival, or at worst portrayed as a sign of insanity. This is demonstrated in an episode in season 4 of AMC's *The Walking Dead* entitled "the Grove." A short exchange takes place between Carol Peletier, one of the survivors, and a teenage girl, Lizzie Samuels. Lizzie asks Carol to reminisce about her daughter, Sophia, who went missing, died, and turned into a zombie. After hearing Carol's praise for Sophia's innocence and gentleness—Carol remarks that Sophia "didn't have a mean bone in her body"—Lizzie asks half-rhetorically, "is that why she isn't here now?" This statement is then assented to by Carol with a resigned "Yeah." As an aside, it is noteworthy that the starkest points in *The Walking Dead* are made with reference to children, in particular Sophia, Lizzie, and her sister Mika. These children, signs of hope for renewal in the face of the zombie apocalypse,[52] perish beneath the tsunami

52. Indeed, Thomas Aquinas once remarked in his *Summa Theologica* that youth (and by extension, children) "is a cause of hope. For . . . the future is long and the past is short." See *I, II*, 40, 6. Cited in Pieper, *Faith, Hope, Love* , 108.

of death. Sophia is bitten and becomes a zombie. Lizzie, already rendered insane, stabs Mika to death. Lizzie herself, whose insta-bility is deemed a severe liability for the survivors, is executed by Carol who, in the course of her execution, uses the beauty of the world—in this case, flowers—to distract Lizzie before she is shot. The point to be made by the show in the portrayal of these three children in particular is that all that is good in the world—inno-cence, beauty, gentleness, optimism, happiness—are ultimately temporary distractions from an inexorable path towards wicked-ness, destruction, and death. This makes sense in psychoanalytic terms because, when left to one's own, an authentic life is one that is premised on "an acceptance of the inevitability and finality of death."[53] Desire, so fundamental in the most basic processes of life, is always geared towards a "desire for death, a partial expression of . . . the death drive."[54] Life on earth, to borrow the imagery from Josef Pieper, is one of straddling between "being and nothingness," and being inexorably oriented towards the latter if left on one's own.[55] Natural life unaided by grace will always be the embodi-ment of Heidegger's "being towards death," orienting itself to what Pieper calls the "memories of what is 'no more,'" and ultimately ending in death.[56] Joy will give way to sadness and light will always be snuffed out, rendering true the final line in Psalm 88—"my only companion is the dark."[57]

The Eucharistic liturgy, in having displacement and the breaking up of the body of Christ to be consumed by others, does not ignore this trajectory. Indeed, on the surface it even gives into that trajectory, insofar that the Eucharist is a commemoration of Christ's death, as Paul reminds us.[58] However, the Eucharist ulti-mately defies the inevitability of death as a terminus, as the very point of the terminus—namely the dispersal and consumption of

---

53. Pound, *Žižek*, 121.

54. Ibid. See also Lacan, *Ecrits*, 719.

55. Pieper, *Faith, Hope, Love*, 96.

56. Ibid., 110.

57. Ps 88:18.

58. 1 Cor 11:26.

Christ's body—becomes the means by which the animated flesh of Christ absorbs and consumes the dead flesh of the consumer. The Eucharist, as Schmemann noted, signals "the end of all natural joy" that one can expect from biological life alone, revealing once and for all "its impossibility, its futility, its sadness."[59] In signaling this threshold of the natural, however, the Eucharist also shows Christ the true man, a man who absorbs natural man into the supernatural life of the Trinity, the supernatural realm in which true joy is to be found. The Eucharist signals that happiness comes not through the effort of humanity, but is a *gift* from God through Christ, who in his wisdom chose death and the darkness of the tomb as the gateway to light and happiness. The Eucharist thus challenges the inevitability the lordship of darkness and sadness, embodying the verse in Psalm 30 which says "weeping may last for the night, but joy comes with the morning."[60]

Indeed, Schmemann takes up the juxtaposition of darkness and night as the backdrop through which the Eucharist gives life through death. Schmemann gives great significance to the fact that the liturgical rituals also implicate a liturgical calendar, the days of which begin not with the sunrise, as it is in the natural calendar, but with evening prayers at sunset, when the day which frames natural life, comes to an end.[61] This follows the sequence in the first creation account, wherein the day is framed with the words "evening came and morning came."[62] The entry into darkness— and with it, the entry into the end of life—is the indispensable start of the liturgical journey. Schmemann adds, however, that it is in how a day *ends* that one comes to learn about that day's "pattern and meaning."[63] From the liturgical standpoint, this entry into darkness or the end of life in the world is not a mourning of a world that has ended. Schmemann speaks of the liturgical evening as a beginning, a "rediscovery, in adoration and thanksgiving, of

---

59. Schmemann, *For the Life of the World*, 54.

60. Ps 30:4.

61. Schmemann, *For the Life of the World*, 59.

62. Gen 1:5.

63. Schmemann, *For the Life of the World*, 60.

the world."[64] The liturgical actions, including those of the Eucharist, unearth the world as it truly is and bring that into our view. And the liturgical world is one that ends in the daylight, brimming with life, newness, and with it, joy. Thus, the true meaning and pattern of the world from the liturgical standpoint is not one in which death is the inevitable terminus. Rather, it is life, joy, and beauty that truly structure the universe and these are so fundamental to the universe that, in Christ, not even death can obliterate them.

It must be reiterated, however, that this pattern of the world as inherently joyous is not a production of humanity. Humanity participates in the production but as it is a liturgical action, it is an action of the church and thus an action of the body of Christ, who is at once full divinity and humanity. It is through the liturgical action of Eucharist that Christ brings our vision beyond the tragic circumstance of the death of night to the comic end of the final victory of life and light of day. To quote Schmemann again, the whole liturgical action is one in which "the Church takes us . . . to that first evening on which [the old Adam] . . . opened his eyes and saw what God in His love was giving to him, saw all the beauty, all the glory . . . and rendered thanks to God. And in this thanksgiving he *became* himself."[65] It is through Christ, the new Adam, who restores this "Eucharistic life"—the life which is framed by the Eucharistic logic of handing over oneself to and for the life of others and which transforms both the universe and our vision of it—that we may see the true comic structure of the cosmos.[66]

---

64. Ibid.

65. Ibid.

66. For a fuller exposition of liturgical action bringing into clearer relief the comic structure of the life in Christ, see Bader-Saye, "Figuring Time," 91–111.

4

The Stations of the Cross
and Christ's Zombification

Introduction

THE PREVIOUS CHAPTERS CONSIDERED how the structure of the Eucharist and the ecclesiology of Christ's body correct the logic of zombie ecclesiology. Going further, the previous chapters considered how the body of Christ not only juxtaposes itself with the zombie horde, but also redeems the body of the zombie. It was argued that the body of Christ reorients the trajectory and logic of consumption and ultimately resists the zombie's proclamation of the inevitability of death as the fundamental orientation of the universe.

Though the above accounts of the zombie and their redemption might sound intellectually satisfying, readers might experience a disconnect with their own life of prayer. This may be even more acute for those more accustomed to traditional forms of devotion, who may find next to no association between their prayer life and the more contemporary forms of pop cultural analysis. This book asserts that such a disconnect between traditional prayer and contemporary social analysis need not be an inevitability. With this in mind, this final chapter will make the analysis of the previous chapters interface with a medieval form devotion, the Stations of the Cross or the *Via Crucis,* or a truncated version thereof. The purpose of this exercise will be twofold. First, because the *Via Crucis* records the concrete steps of the passage of Christ from life to death, it is hoped that such an exercise can further the analysis of the previous chapters by unveiling the way Christ's displacement of his body and his assuming and redeeming of the zombie condition, is operationalized. Secondly, because the *Via Crucis* is an exercise in personal contemplation of these steps, it is also hoped that such an exercise will also draw the reader to make as his or her own the drama of that displacement, assumption, and redemption of the zombie since, as was previously argued, *we* are the zombie.

This chapter has condensed the *Via Crucis* from the original fourteen stations into eight stations, as the repetition of some stations and the striking similarities between others may make an analysis of each and every station redundant. While readers may disagree with this rationalization of stations, it must be noted that the purpose for such a rationalization is purely heuristic, and the primary purpose of the chapter is designed to paint with broad brush strokes the drama of the zombification of Christ. In particular, the focus of this chapter is to demonstrate the redemption of the zombie outlined in the previous chapter, and the process of Jesus' handing over *himself* to assume the implications of *our* human/ zombie condition. The number of stations, therefore, is a secondary concern to the exchange taking place between Jesus and the crowd in each step of Jesus' passion, and the process of Christ's zombification that occurs as the Christ takes on *our* zombified condition.

The *Via Crucis* with Zombie Jesus

Jesus Is Condemned to Die

This station records Christ's condemnation by the governor of Judea, Pontius Pilate, to be taken out of the city and crucified.[1] This first station is significant, not only because it initiates the Way

1. John 19:12–16.

of the Cross, but also because this station acts as a compendium of the other stations in a number of important ways. In the first instance, there is the foretaste of death. The kind of death Jesus is condemned to is twofold. In sentencing Jesus to be nailed to a cross, there is the obvious physical death to which he is condemned. However, as alluded to in the previous chapters, there is another, subtler death to which Jesus is condemned. For crucifixion is a death that occurs outside the community—indeed the fact that Jesus is taken out of the city for his execution is recorded in the Gospels.[2] The victim of crucifixion not only suffers the death of his flesh, but also the death of isolation, of being stricken from the living flesh of a social body.

What the reader sees in this station is the continuation of the process of the displacement of Christ body that we have seen in pre-passion episodes, such as in the healing of the man with the skin disease. We also saw this displacement in sacramental form at the Lord's Supper, where Christ handed his body over to the custody of his disciples. In that Eucharistic starting point his body, identified with the Eucharistic elements, becomes broken to be consumed by his disciples. This process of relinquishing custody of his body over to that of others is continuing on the process of handing over of the body of Christ to the custody of the authorities in Judea. This first station depicts a process initiated by Jesus' willing handing over of himself, a handing over that sets in train a process of destabilizing his body, dispersing it and feeding it to a zombified horde. This is a horde that has been deadened by sin. As the Old Testament reminds us, the social body among which the body of Jesus walked is a body deadened by many episodes of idolatry, that is, the worship of gods other than the God of Israel, and in particular the worship of the self as its own Messiah. The prophet Ezekiel vividly encapsulates how the flesh of this social body comes to die from its idolatry. Chief among its effects is the tearing at the flesh of the social body through separation as the House of Israel "is scattered . . . among the nations and . . .

---

2. John 19:17.

dispersed throughout the countries."[3] This comes through a civil war between Israel and Judah, and the resultant killing of kinfolk by kinfolk, and it comes through imperial conquest from the powers of the Near East, and then finally by Rome. In addition to the separation of flesh from the social body, the prophet Ezekiel outlines also how the flesh that remains becomes necrotic from this idolatry. On the outside, it has become covered with filth,[4] while on the inside, the flesh has been robbed of its spirit. It has been turned into the unanimated flesh of *sarx*, such that the core of this flesh—its heart—has been turned to stone.[5] The prophet Micah gives an additional chilling note of the effects of idolatry, in which God finds the House of Israel as a zombie horde, "skinning people alive, pulling the flesh off their bones, eating [His] people's flesh."[6] Even the land on which this social body treads has been zombified. Not only is it devoid of life from its not bearing any harvests, but it is also turned into a "man-eater," robbing "a nation of its children." Both land and people have become zombified, deadened not only through their own physical neglect, but also in verbal assault via "enduring the insults of the nations."[7]

To the zombified horde that eats God's people's flesh, the Son of God now hands over his body to be dispersed and fed on. In doing so, Christ takes their place, as noted in the Markan analysis above, and Christ is turned into a zombie by the crowd. The way to understand this zombification by a zombified horde is to see how the process of displacing Christ's body continues on in the phase between the end of the Lord's Supper and his condemnation by Pilate. For Christ's dispersal of his body continues well after the Last Supper. It continues in the Garden of Gethsemane, when blood drips from the brow of Jesus onto the ground. Christ blood is mingled in with the ground that they call "man-eater." The displacement of Jesus continues with his being bound and manhandled by

3. Ezek 36:19.
4. Ezek 36:25.
5. Ezek 36:26.
6. Mic 3:2.
7. Ezek 36:7.

the representatives of the "chief priests and elders of the people."[8] His displacement continues on in the verbal assault consisting in his interrogation by the Sanhedrin, with his reputation being undermined by false witnesses. His displacement continues on in his scourging, with his flesh torn and his scalp crushed and shredded by thorns. His displacement continues when Pilate proclaims "behold the man" and presents that battered and humiliated body to the crowd.

Only, this is no ordinary crowd. This crowd is Jerusalem, the City of God. This is the city whereby one experiences the transcendent, by virtue of the presence of the temple. This is where, as it says in the Psalms, "the tribes go up."[9] And yet, this is the very city where the zombified are put on full display. For despite the prophets' calls back to the recognition of the transcendence grounded in the true worship of God, what ended up being enacted by the ascent of the "tribes of the Lord" was the haughty idea that humanity can take the place of God, exercising the prerogative that is due only to Him, and thus acting wilfully without regard to any higher authority than our own desires. Thus, this crowd is no ordinary crowd, but a crowd that wanted to access the "death drive," seeking their own immortality and ending up necrotic. Wanting to become angels, this crowd is now a crowd of zombies.

As covered in previous chapters, subjectivity and identity are erased within the zombified horde. Those within it are referred to in collective terms, such as "we," "they," and "all the people." In this collective designation, or—indeed in any linguistic marker—every person in this crowd has, as Lacan puts it, "lost [him/herself] . . . as an object."[10] The crowd is not satisfied to see the shredded body of Jesus put before them. The crowd wants more, to feed a desire to dominate, a bloodlust that sin generates within each of us. In their own way, the crowd seek to consume Jesus and incorporate him into the horde. In acting on this bloodlust, this horde of zombies does not produce the indistinct gurgle that one is familiar with

8. Matt 26:47.

9. Ps 122:4.

10. Lacan, *Ecrits*, 247.

in the movies and television programs. Nonetheless, the collective cry of these zombies is indicative of both their bloodlust and their inability to do little more than conform to the horde: "Crucify him!" That this is the "death drive" at work is indicated by the lack of concern of any adverse consequences of their request. At the warning that Pilate relinquishes himself of responsibility for Jesus' death, the horde take that culpability onto themselves with the cry "His blood be on us an on our children!"[11]

With their cry of "Crucify him!" the horde call for a Roman form of execution to feed their bloodlust. With this cry Jerusalem, the city of urban angels, implicate another city, the city of pagan Rome, to participate in the process of zombification. In a way, they already have participated in their active role in the torture of Jesus. They have actually turned what was the most beautiful body into a moving heap of shredded skin and flesh. With a single cry Rome, an empire, the center of the all of the known world, is being pulled into this feeding frenzy of the flesh of the Savior, which is then played out in the following stations.

Jesus Takes Up His Cross

Before beginning this station, recall that at every point from the Eucharist on, Jesus engages in a displacing of his body. In so displacing his body, Jesus completes the assumption of the condition of those to whom he was sent. This is the condition of the zombie horde and, in so displacing his body, Jesus himself assumes the condition of the zombie. We have seen from the previous station that Jesus already begins to assume the dimensions of the zombie through his torture, his condemnation, and his ousting from the community. Now the process of Jesus' zombification continues with the taking up of his cross. The question to be raised here is: how can this cross that Jesus takes onto his shoulders speak to our analysis of the previous chapters?

---

11. Matt 27:24–25.

At one level, the cross is an instrument of power projection by the empire and, thus, it is a symbol of the known world, the center of which is a city. Moreover, this is no ordinary world, it is a world encapsulated by a symbol of execution. The cross thereby stands as a subtle indictment of imperial power, where such power is maintained by having the threat of death hanging over the world. Using this threat of death the empire as a city can, through the cross, act as a stand-in for the transcendence sought by humanity, whereby one tries to transcend others through the exertion of expansive power. Augustine's idea of the lust for domination pulsating through the city of man resonates strongly here, for the empire is a city and Jerusalem is a cipher for the city of Rome—recall that the crowd in Jerusalem declared their king to be Caesar. Indeed, they have "no king but Caesar."[12] At the same time, the cross also signifies the competitive aspect of this imperial manifestation of the "death drive" as transcendence-through-domination, since the cross is a tool of punishment for those that try to challenge our pretensions of being higher in the social ladder than all others— higher than others in this urban angelic order. As Pickstock has pointed out, however, this is a transcendence that is purely *of this world* and, as such, this immanent transcendence will always end up necrophilic. The cross perfectly encapsulates the necrophilic logic of transcendence through temporal power leading unto death. In a word, the cross is the icon of a zombified world. This zombified world is that which Jesus takes up onto his shoulders. Even as he suffers the zombification of torture and isolation, he knows he has to bear the weight of the entire world's zombification onto his body. This is the weight he must now carry through and out of the streets of Jerusalem.

This carrying of the cross of our zombification through the streets of Jerusalem is an important component of our salvation. For salvation is not a gnostic assent to an idea, nor is it a Pelegian system of behaviors to attain our own salvation. The first Passover, recorded in the book of Exodus,[13] reminds us that our salvation

12. John 19:15.
13. Exod 12:1–14.

comes not from our ascent to God, but by God's descent and passing through the world of humanity. In the incarnate Word, salvation is not just constituted by God passing through humanity, but is passing *through* humanity in the human named Jesus of Nazareth. Salvation is walking *through* the city of man and in doing so, gathering up the flesh that sin has consumed and scattered. Moreover, salvation is handing over himself to us in that passage, and then his carrying back what was handed over back to himself. Our salvation is a procession of the Son, walking through the earth, carrying a cross of the world's zombification, back to the Father.

This walk through the streets of the city is a walk that leads to one's death. At the same time, it is what God has shown to be the path of life. On this road to the Place of the Skull lies the path to the fulfillment of the "death drive." In psychoanalytic terms, this is sheer madness. The paradox identified by psychoanalysis, however, is that it is precisely in this madness of abnegation that the ground of all reality can be established.[14] More specifically, it is in the madness of moving towards one's death that one knows what it means to be fully alive as a human being.[15] More specifically still, it is the madness of the incarnate Word moving to his own death that sets the stage for the possibility of life for everyone. For it is Jesus of Nazareth who said that he came so that we might have life to the full[16] and that the way of life is a path of discipleship, the centerpiece of which is taking up his cross and following him.[17] And as shall be demonstrated below, it is in this path of Jesus' own zombification that he is also showing us the path to a true immortality, a true fulfillment of the "death drive."

---

14. Žižek, *The Žižek Reader*, 259.

15. Pound, *Žižek: A (Very) Critical Introduction*, 31.

16. John 10:10.

17. Matt 16:24; Luke 9:23.

Jesus Meets His Mother and the Women of Jerusalem

In previous stations we see Christ becoming zombified, assuming the condition of the zombies that we have become. Though this be the case, Jesus nonetheless refuses to give into the zombie, as mentioned above. The Father fulfils the promise in Psalm 16 by never leaving His Son among the dead nor allow His body to see corruption.[18] For even as the Son stumbles through the cobblestones of Jerusalem to what will be his death beyond its walls, this very same path is also the path that is brimming with life. Traditionally, Jesus will meet his mother and later the women of Jerusalem, and in these two separate stations we will see that as Jesus stumbles to his death, we catch glimmers of the redemption of the zombie.

As was mentioned in the first station, the process of redemption brings back together the flesh that sin had torn apart, a bringing together that is brought through the encounter between the zombified masses and the zombified Christ. We see a glimpse of this process of redemption through the encounter between Christ and his mother. Note, for instance, how this is the first station in which someone in Jerusalem apart from Jesus is given a distinct identity as a subject. In the Catholic tradition, Mary, though human, has nonetheless been distinguished from the zombified masses through God's intervention, by being protected by God from sin from the moment of her conception.[19] So though human and amidst the zombie horde in the *Via Crucis*, Mary nonetheless never disappears into it to become just another zombie. This is confirmed by Christ's meeting with her as the first distinct subject. In isolation, this meeting might at first glance not have any meaningful bearing on the process of Jesus' saving of the human race from the zombie, since Mary does not share the distinct feature of a zombified race, namely sin. But recall from previous chapters that Jesus exposes sin to be an aberration of the human condition, not the indispensable norm. Mary thus is a part of this humanity,

18. Ps 16:10.

19. This was definitively articulated by Pope Pius IX in the 1854 papal bull *Ineffabilis Deus.*

but not in its zombified form. Mary also has the distinction given to her by the early church fathers, from Justin Martyr onwards, of being a "Second Eve." And it is due not to any special status on her part, but because of the saving power of God. Mary is thus human, but she is also the prototype of a humanity saved from its sin by Christ.[20] Thus, Mary's subjectivity is a subjectivity restored in Christ. In this station we see a faint glimmer of hope in this process of Jesus' zombification, because we are given the chance to see the endpoint of the process of the redemption of the zombie. It is significant that Christ saving work and Mary's displaying the effects of that work can be encapsulated in this encounter. It is an encounter where no words are recorded. There is nothing but the sheer presence of Christ before one of God's creatures. More than any word or signifier, it is this presence of the incarnate *Logos*, the ground of all being, that in turn brings what Conor Cunningham calls "being . . . [that is] the beyond of thought."[21] Jesus saves all creatures in the way he saves Mary, through a restoration of the profundity of a creature's being, which goes beyond the reductiveness of *sarx*. Only the presence of Christ's *soma* can properly articulate the profundity of what is to be bestowed onto creatures by God. In so doing, God saves by restoring the self back to the self.[22]

Jesus' encounter with Mary is juxtaposed with the second encounter with the weeping women of Jerusalem, recorded in the Gospel of Luke.[23] In this encounter, we see sadness on full display. For this is a sadness that sees no end beyond destruction and

20. The joint Anglican and Roman Catholic International Commission declaration on Mary, *Mary: Grace and Hope in Christ*, demonstrates how this saving power of Christ encompasses Mary as well as the human race. In the case of Mary, Christ's saving work "reached back in Mary to the depths of her being and to her earliest beginnings." See Anglican-Roman Catholic International Commission, *Mary, Grace and Hope in Christ*, 59.

21. Cunningham, *Genealogy of Nihilism*, 260.

22. Pound, *Žižek: A (Very) Critical Introduction*, 99.

23. "And following him was a large crowd of the people, and of women who were mourning and lamenting him. But Jesus turning to them said, "Daughters of Jerusalem, do not weep for me, but weep for yourselves and for your children." See Luke 23:27–28.

death—specifically the destruction and death of Jesus—and as argued in the chapters above, a sadness that turns towards death is a sadness constitutive of the zombified condition. This is indicated by the fact that, in contrast to Mary's clear identification as a subject, the women of Jerusalem wail as an indistinct collective. We are unable to distinguish one woman from another. These women may be different from the rest of the zombified masses, in that they do not desire the torn flesh of Jesus, but want to express a sympathy and sadness for that flesh. Even that sympathy, however, is expressed as a zombified mass, and what good they desire must swirl within that of the zombified mass. This link between their sadness and the zombified masses is indicated by Jesus' word to these women to weep, not for him, but for "yourselves and your children." With these words, Jesus is engaging in an act of displacement of his body, an act of exchange between his flesh and that of the women. For with these words, Jesus receives weeping and wailing, takes it upon himself, and engages in the Eucharistic exchange to the women's place among the zombified. The first fruits of this exchange are far more subtle than those seen in the encounter with Mary, because the first fruits of this exchange are indicated by an identifier of "daughters." Though they are a collective, they are nonetheless being given an identity that distinguishes them from the zombified horde. They are being taken from the nameless mass and being taken together as members of a family. We thus in a single movement, see the fulfillment of the psalm that says "the Lord heals the broken hearted, he binds up all their wounds."[24] However, the full fruits of this exchange is still yet to be seen, for recall that even as linguistic identifiers can distinguish one part of a mass from another, Lacan argues that they still lack subjectivity. The women of Jerusalem, in being locked in a linguistic signifier, are yet to be fully restored. Through these encounters with the women, both Mary and the daughters of Jerusalem, we see that the Eucharistic exchange is yet to be fully realized and its fruits yet to be fully experienced.

24. Ps 147:3.

Jesus Falls Three Times

When Jesus takes up his cross, he does so already zombified, with his physical body torn and his place in the social body stricken from him. The taking up of the cross of a zombified culture, that symbol of the death drive, which attempt at transcendence yet which collapses into death, is but another step of his taking our place in this culture. In this station we see not one but three times in which the weight of a human-driven transcendence is demonstrated to be not a path to reach the lofty heights of transcendence, but a burden that bears down to crush bodies, enacting the "horror of the flesh" in postmodern culture that Juvin wrote about. In these stations we come to see the zombified Christ putting on full display that burden, falling under the crushing weight, not just of the cross, but of humanity's ambition to be godlike without God. And under that ambition, skin tears, flesh bruises, and bones crack. In this station we witness what the "necrophilia" identified by Pickstock looks like.

Here we see a visceral sign that Jesus, the God-made-man, has truly displaced his body into the world, and has taken our place in it. In his incarnation, he has taken on our flesh. As we saw in the exchange with the man with the skin disease in the Gospel of Mark, we see in his public ministry the displacing of his *soma* and exchanging it for our *sarx*. In his fall to the ground under the weight of the cross, we see Jesus exhibiting the limits of our *sarx*. Jesus is showing the utter inability of *sarx* to bear the weight of infinite expectations borne out of the death drive. As crushing as that may be, there is another vivid display taking place, for while Jesus falls, he does not stay fallen. This is because Jesus the incarnate Word is not the dead flesh of *sarx*, but the animated flesh of *soma*, brimming with real divine life, as opposed to the simulated divinity of postmodern culture, the simulated infinity that comes with acting on the "death drive." Furthermore, as Ward reminded us earlier, Jesus' dispersal of his flesh to assume our *sarx* does not lead to an annihilation of the Lord's *soma*. In Jesus, we see Jesus' *soma* co-abiding with our *sarx*, and it is only through that divine life in the *soma* of Christ that we are able to bear the sheer force of the world's pretensions to god-likeness. Christ's flesh refuses to be crushed under the oppression of the crosses the world puts on our shoulders and calls a better life. This station then, that of Christ's falling under the weight of the cross and getting up again, is a sign for us of the co-abiding in Christ that Paul speaks of in his letter to the Galatians when, after speaking of living through the sufferings that might kill him, he declares that "it is not [he] that lives, but Christ who lives in [him]."[25]

Before concluding that this is a display of Christian machismo, note this key difference. Jesus' refusal of death does not mean a throwing off of the cross. Rather, the one brimming with the life of *soma embraces* the cross. With every time that Jesus gets up, he continues to hold onto the means of his death. In this he shows us that the life of *soma* is not a gnostic casting off of *sarx*. The paradox that Jesus puts before us is that it is through the endpoint of *sarx*—death—that the life of *soma* comes. For even though death remains on this earth, it no longer has supremacy because of its being absorbed into the flesh of Christ. This station is a sign that it is through the handing over of one's flesh to the zombified that the zombie is redeemed, and it is precisely insofar as this handing over is done against the backdrop of the animated flesh of Christ that our dying flesh can, with this handing over, avoid the inevitability of necrophilia and its commitment to the supremacy of death.

Simon and Veronica Assist Jesus

In stations where other people are identified, we see Jesus taking on and redeeming the zombified horde. In the traditional rendition of the Stations of the Cross, in two separate stations, two individuals other than Mary are identified by name, namely Simon of Cyrene and a mysterious woman named Veronica. For heuristic purposes, these two have been put into the same station in this book. What is significant in these two individuals is that, in them, we see yet

25. Gal 2:20.

another aspect of Jesus' redemptive work, the extension of the process of handing over to the other parts of the body of Christ. We also see in these stations the sheer scope of the displacement of his body and identify lessons in how we, who participate in and are displaced by the Eucharistic displacement of his body, must now also ourselves displace our bodies in our lives in the world, with the cross and the battered body of Christ as our indispensable touchstones.

Consider first Simon of Cyrene. The Scriptural accounts do not make clear if Simon was a Jew, but the designation of "the Cyrenean" indicates something very important. Simon is a foreigner, cut off from the life of the holy city of Jerusalem. Simon is one of the zombified, pulled by the zombified mob into the epicentre of the Way of the Cross. This action of being pulled from the margins of a watching public to the cross, shows the continuity between the zombified mass watching Jesus and the weight of the cross itself. The Cyrenean then suffers the kicks and insults as he carries the cross for Jesus. If one were to visualize this action, one might notice the distinction between the zombie and Jesus breaking down and our pretensions to distinguish the zombified horde from us good Christians similarly beginning to break down. The breakdown of this distinction, however, between the redeemer and those to be redeemed does not lead to a dissolution of the body of Christ. In carrying the cross, Simon is no longer just another bystander in a faceless crowd. He is designated not just as another indistinct man from Cyrene, but is given the life of a subject, indicated by the articulation of a name, Simon. Thus, in Simon's bearing of the cross of Christ, Simon is no longer a zombie, for he is being given life from his identification with Jesus and his cross. To paraphrase one of Jesus' sayings in the Synoptic Gospels, in Simon's losing of his life—which was only an illusion of a life anyway—for the sake of bearing the cross of Jesus, Simon found true life, signified by his identification as a subject.

A similar story could be said of Veronica who, in a separate station, wipes the face of Jesus. Veronica appears nowhere in the Scriptures, and thus has the status of an invisible figure in the

Scriptural accounts. Like the Cyrenean, Veronica also suffers the anonymity of the zombified. However, in the lived memory of the church through the ages, especially in the Stations of the Cross, Veronica is taken out of that anonymity. Her identity is made known to us through this station by the church, by the body of Christ. Like the Cyrenean, Veronica also comes into direct contact with the broken body of Christ. In so doing, like the Cyrenean, Veronica would also have faced the harassment of the zombified masses that are in turn harrying Jesus. In being close to Jesus' body, whether in the physical or in the mystical body of the church, Veronica has her own zombification redeemed through Christ's own zombification. Her dead flesh is animated by that of Christ, and she now bears the *soma* of Christ in her *sarx*, which is demonstrated in the image of Christ being present on the items of her perishable life, on the cloth that she might have used for everyday life. In this little act of imprinting his image on Veronica's facial cloth, we see a small glimpse of the sheer scope of Jesus' redemption of the zombified. His saving work is not confined to just physical flesh, but extends to "make all things new," to borrow from the book of the Apocalypse.[26] The work of the body of Christ extends to cover bodies—physical, social, cultural, and indeed the whole cosmos, with nothing being left untouched. Indeed, we see in this part of the Stations of the Cross a sign of the impending fulfillment of Christ's prediction in the Gospel of John that he will draw all things to himself.[27]

Jesus Is Stripped of His Garments

Having extended Jesus' body among the zombified crowds of Jerusalem and beyond, and having taken their place among horde by taking their zombification upon himself, an already zombified Christ has now arrived at Golgotha. The zombification of Christ, however, has still not yet reached its crescendo. More must still

26. Rev 21:5.
27. John 12:32.

be undertaken by Jesus and we see in this station a furthering of his zombification coming in another form of tearing and consuming the flesh of Christ by the zombified mob. In this station, Jesus continues the process of handing over his body. In some renditions of the Stations, mention is made of opened flesh sticking to Jesus' clothing, with wounds being reopened once these are divested of Jesus' body. While the Romans actively tear at the flesh of Jesus by stripping him, naked flesh is also put on full display for the visual consumption of the zombified horde who have been baying for his blood all the way from the heart of the holy city of Jerusalem to well beyond its walls.

Note an important inversion taking place here. What is put on full display for the consumption of the crowds is not the angelic flesh of a model, but the battered, bruised, and shredded flesh of a monster. Having taken on the condition of the zombified, the stripped Zombie Jesus has put the result of that zombification— our monstrosity—in full view. Putting the results of their desire for flesh before their eyes, however, does not break the circuit of that desire. Rather, having the flesh of Zombie Jesus on display has furthered the turning of the body of Christ into a product for consumption, not just of the gaze of the zombified mob, but also as a thing to be gambled with by the Romans.[28] In this station, another facet of the salvation of the zombified is revealed. Not only is the body of Jesus handed over to the mob, not only is Jesus taking on our zombified condition. In doing all of these, Jesus fulfils his promise made in the Gospel of Matthew of "utter[ing] what has been hidden since the foundation of the world."[29] At one level, he reveals the monstrosity of the process of zombification, since it is through the actions and will of the zombified horde that the naked body and torn flesh of Christ now stands before them. Yet, precisely because the dissemination of the flesh of Christ among the horde does not result in the disappearance of the former into the latter, Zombie Jesus stripped of his garments and flesh reveals in that very torn flesh, that all-important threshold between death

28. John 19:24.
29. Matt 13:35.

and life, where previously there was none beyond the inexorable path towards death.

Jesus Is Nailed to and Dies on the Cross

In this station, Jesus' assuming the condition of a zombie is brought to its climax. Here, Jesus is not only carrying the symbols of the "death drive"—the cross—but also becomes inextricably bound to it. Jesus' bond to the death drive, however, is anything but organic. It is as artificial as it is brutal. The nailing of Jesus to the cross continues yet again the process of Jesus' dissemination of his flesh, as not just his flesh but joints now become rendered—an extra-biblical account states that one of his arms was pulled till it was dislocated from the shoulder in order to fit his arms on the cross. If true, it would give voice the brutal artificiality of the death drive in contemporary times, as bodies become broken to fit the pre-set requirements of the postmodern angel, as flesh and bone become cut to enact the death drive swirling within consumer culture, embodied in furniture, skin-tight clothing, diets, and plastic surgery. The hands and feet of Zombie Jesus, having been stretched by the nails and held in place, once again put on display how the death drive leads to nothing but one's death.

At his crucifixion, Zombie Jesus' assumption of our zombified condition comes to its climax. This moment fulfills Paul's second letter to the Corinthians, where "God made him who knew no sin to become sin to become sin on our behalf, so that we might become the righteousness of God."[30] For if the zombie is the emblem of sin, then the Jesus hanging on the cross is truly the zombified Christ. One clue to this is at the level of Jesus' relationship to God the Father. In the Gospel of John, Jesus declares in one place that he does not do his own will, but that of the Father who sent him,[31] indicating a subordination of himself to the Father. In another place, Jesus declares the degree of his intimacy with the Father,

30. 2 Cor 5:21.
31. John 4:34.

saying that he "and the Father are one."[32] The identity of Jesus is inextricably grounded in his identification with the Father. Furthermore, it is that very identification with the Father that paves the way to his crucifixion by the zombified mob, a mob that erases identity from each and everyone. And on that cross Zombie Jesus, having taken on our sinful zombified condition, loses the grounds of his identity, his identification with the Father. This is expressed in his cry of dereliction, an important moment for Žižek, but for the exact opposite reason. It is significant because it is here that Jesus finds his identity apart from God, which Žižek celebrates as a positive development. Jesus does not say the familial term borne out of the privilege of sonship, *Abba,* the term he used just before his passion, in Gethsemane.[33] Zombie Jesus on the Cross, having borne the sin of all and thus its concomitant separation from God and the loss of familial intimacy, cries out instead a cry of the abandoned to their deity, "My God, my God!"[34] On the cross, Zombie Jesus truly identifies with the horde, having been made just one of the people over whom God stands aloof.

Again, as indicated in the previous station, Jesus' handing over of his body to the horde is not a surrender to the ultimate sovereignty of death. What Jesus does in assuming the condition of a zombie is not to legitimize the horde or the lordship of death it embodies. What Zombie Jesus does is redeem the death drive, and in that redemption become the threshold between death and life, and more importantly the gateway from death to life. In his zombified body lies the meeting point between *sarx* and *soma,* where the dead receive new and everlasting life. But this gateway to life is in this station a dripping mess of shredded skin and flesh. Nailed to the cross, there is no other way possible for his body to move, outside of being inextricably bound to a platform built solely for death.

Even here, however, we see the extension of his body through his word. For Jesus is *the* Word that has become flesh, and we recall every time we say the Nicene Creed that it is through the Word

32. John 6:38.

33. Mark 14:36.

34. Matt 27:46.

that all things are made. What this means is that, even as his body is bound to the cross—the symbol of death—we continue to see the dissemination of that body via the utterance of his words, words from which new life springs. We see new life in the new family that he creates with Mary and the Beloved Disciple—Behold your mother! Behold Your Son![35]—and we see new life in the gateway to paradise that the words of Zombie Jesus open for the repentant thief—You will be with me in paradise.[36] Finally, we see new life when Zombie Jesus, standing at the threshold of death, gives new life to the entire universe when, having assumed the entirety of the human condition and united himself with the whole world and entered death, he hands the universe over to its transcendent Creator with the words of a Son—"Father, into your hands, I commend my spirit!"[37] Instead of permanently abandoning his dependence on the Father, as Žižek would like to have it, Zombie Jesus instead prays a line from Psalm 31, where the author not only commends his spirit, but does so depending upon God's delivery.[38] Having initially lost his identity with the Father by entering the pseudo-immortality of the death drive, Jesus opens up the way to real immortality by lifting up the whole world—which recall was absorbed into his displaced body—and offering it in a Eucharistic fashion back to its Creator. Having bound himself to the zombified condition of the world and then having offered up that world to be delivered from its fate by its Creator, Zombie Jesus regains his identification with his Father. We see the signs of this Eucharistic action bringing life to a dead universe by the fact that death becomes transcended no sooner after his own entry into death. Death no longer becomes the inevitable terminus for the universe. Recall that after Jesus' bearing the burden of zombification which ends in death, and having delivered the human condition from the

35. John 19:26–27.
36. Luke 23:43.
37. Luke 23:46.
38. Ps 31:5.

inevitability of death, the dead rose from their graves and moved among the inhabitants of Jerusalem.[39]

Jesus Is Taken Down and Buried

In this stage of the Way of the Cross, the process of Jesus' zombification is consummated. Having handed over himself and exchanged places with the horde, we have seen how in each station of the Way of the Cross, Jesus assumed the condition of the zombie at differing levels. Jesus stared the zombie in the face and did not destroy the zombie in the tradition set by popular culture—with a violent blow to the head. Instead, Jesus takes on its condition and becomes Zombie Jesus for our sakes. In doing so Jesus himself becomes the victim of a blow to the head through his crown of thorns, a blow to the body through his torture and carrying the cross, a blow to the psyche through insult and spittle, then a blow to the soul through Jerusalem's expulsion and his separation from God. Instead of violently interrupting humankind's pretensions of creating god-likeness without God, a process that ends in the rotting stench of death, Jesus took those pretensions onto himself and allowed himself to stink of death. At each stage of the Stations of the Cross, and at the place of the skull Jesus embodied the "death drive" of humankind and put its results on full display for everyone to see. However, in so embracing the "death drive," Zombie Jesus also continued the Eucharistic logic of handing over his body. Myriad wonderful things were put into effect because of Christ's extension of his body, and then through every stage of his passion, and on the cross. With every beating, with every whipping, with every insult, with every drop of blood splattered and with every bit of flesh strewn across the streets of Jerusalem, Christ's body was being Eucharistically fractioned and distributed to be consumed by the zombified masses, and like a giant net Christ's body enveloped all of that very creation that sought to consume him.

39. Matt 27:52.

At this point of the Way of the Cross, however, with only a dead body of Christ to behold, those miniscule comforts witnessed in the previous stations seem like mere distractions to the visceral reality of flesh being torn from Christ. On the cross, and later on the lap of his mother, the only thing that the reader can consider a given is nothing more than a corpse. The "death drive" of humankind, instead of being the path to an abundance of life, has brought us to a decisive cadaveric end. In this station, we seem to hear the echo of the insult by the chief priests, the teachers of the law and the elders, "He saved others and he cannot save himself."[40] There is a sting when a teacher of the law speaks of the futility of Jesus' actions. In a certain respect, there is an element of truth to it. Remember that in the letters of Paul, such as in Romans 8:3, Paul always associated the old Law with the weakness of human flesh, which was why he says in that letter that the old Law could not save us. Thus, in the Law of the flesh, any acting on the "death drive" would be futile and death would thus spell the end.

It is at the very point when things have come to an end, however, that Schmemann provides a hopeful reminder. This Way of the Cross is not an ordinary execution, but a liturgical act. It is a Eucharistic act, set in a liturgical schema of time. As we witness the dead body of Jesus on the lap of his mother, as we see the body of Jesus being taken, wrapped up, and put into a tomb, we see in the Gospel of Matthew that night is about to fall.[41] But as the book of Genesis via Schmemann reminds us, the night of evening has come but the day has not yet ended. Seen in the light of the Liturgy, death is only the beginning.[42] Death is yet to give way to the newness of life that comes with the morning. The new life that comes with that light may not come with the passage of that very evening, or the evening after that, but Jesus has given us enough clues in his own zombification that the tsunami of death that the zombie embodies is not the world's endgame. In the silence of the tomb,

40. Matt 27:42.

41. Matt 27:57.

42. Schmemann, *For the Life of the World*, 51.

the dead body of Jesus seems to whisper to us the words that the prophet Isaiah once said

> "See now, I am doing a new thing. Look there, it springs up. Can you not see it already?"[43]

43. Isa 43:19.

Bibliography

Anglican-Roman Catholic International Commission. In *Mary, Grace and Hope in Christ: The Seattle Statement of the Anglican-Roman Catholic International Commission*, edited by Donald Bolen and Gregory Cameron, 7–88. New York: Continuum, 2007.

Augustine. *Confessions*. Translated by Henry Chadwick. Oxford: Oxford University Press, 1991.

Bader-Saye, Scott. "Figuring Time: Providence and Politics." In *Liturgy, Time and the Politics of Redemption*, edited by Randi Rashkover Pecknold and C.C, 91–111. Grand Rapids: Eerdmans, 2006.

Badley, Linda. *Film, Horror and the Body Fantastic*. Contributions to the Study of Popular Culture. Westport, CT: Greenwood, 1995.

Balthasar, Hans Urs von. *The Realm of Metaphysics in the Modern Age*. Vol. 5. The Glory of the Lord. Edinburgh: T. & T. Clark, 1991.

Bauman, Zygmunt. *Intimations of Postmodernity*. London: Routledge, 1992.

Bishop, Jeffrey P. *The Anticipatory Corpse: Medicine, Power and the Care of the Dying*. Notre Dame, IN: University of Notre Dame Press, 2011.

Bourdieu, Pierre. *Outline of a Theory of Practice*. Cambridge: Cambridge University Press, 1977.

Bray, Gerald Lewis, and Thomas Oden. *1–2 Corinthians*. 3rd ed. Ancient Christian Commentary on Scripture: New Testament VII. Downers Grove, IL: IVP, 1999.

Castoriadis, Cornelius. "Radical Imagination and the Social Instituting Imaginary." In *The Castoriadis Reader*, edited by David Ames Curtis, 318–37. Oxford: Blackwell, 1997.

Cavanaugh, William T. *Theopolitical Imagination: Discovering the Liturgy as a Political Act in an Age of Global Consumerism*. London: T. & T. Clark, 2004.

Clements, Susannah. *The Vampire Defanged: How the Embodiment of Evil Became a Romantic Hero*. Grand Rapids: Brazos, 2011.

Cunningham, Connor. *Genealogy of Nihilism*. London: Routledge, 2002.

de Certeau, Michel. *The Practice of Everyday Life*. Berkeley: University of California Press, 1984.

Dulles, Avery. "The Ecclesial Dimension of Faith." *Communio: International Catholic Review* 22 (1995) 418–32.

Dunne, John S. *City of the Gods*. London: Sheldon, 1965.

Dunn, James G. *The Theology of Paul the Apostle*. Grand Rapids: Eerdmans, 2006.

Foucault, Michel. *Discipline and Punish*. 2nd ed. New York: Vintage, 1995.

Goodchild, Philip. *Theology of Money*. Durham, NC: Duke University Press, 2009.

Gorringe, Tim J. *A Theology of the Built Environment: Justice, Empowerment, Redemption*. Cambridge: Cambridge University Press, 2004.

Groening, Matt, and David X. Cohen. "When Aliens Attack." *Futurama*, Season 1, Episode 12. Aired 7 November 1999. 21st Century Fox Television 1999.

Guiton, Jacques. *The Ideas of Le Corbusier*. New York: Braziller, 1981.

Guthrie, Steven R. *Creator Spirit: The Holy Spirit and the Art of Becoming Human*. Grand Rapids: Baker Academic, 2011.

Harries, Karsten. *The Ethical Function of Architecture*. Cambridge: MIT Press, 1997.

Hauerwas, Stanley. "Citizens of Heaven." Duke Divinity School, Durham NC, February 28, 2013. https://www.youtube.com/watch?v=HRsWMIaNvnc.

Juvin, Hervé. *The Coming of the Body*. New York: Verso, 2010.

Kasinitz, Philip. *Metropolis: Center and Symbol of Our Times*. London: Macmillan, 1995.

Kendrick, Walter. *In the Thrill of Fear: 250 Years of Scary Entertainment*. New York: Grove, 1991.

Lacan, Jacques. *Ecrits*. Translated by Bruce Fink. New York: Norton, 2006.

———. *The Ego in Freud's Theory and in the Technique of Psychoanlaysis, 1954–1955*. Edited by Jacques-Alain Miller. The Seminar of Jacques Lacan, II. London: Norton, 1991.

Laderman, Gary. *Rest in Peace: A Cultural History of Death and the Funeral Home in 20th Century America*. New York: Oxford University Press, 2003.

Latour, Bruno. *We Have Never Been Modern*. Cambridge: Harvard University Press, 1993.

Laws, Robin D. *40 Years of Gen Con*. St. Paul, MN: Atlas Games, 2007.

Loudermilk, A. "Eating 'Dawn' in the Dark: Zombie Desire and Commodified Identity in George A. Romero's 'Dawn of the Dead.'" *Journal of Consumer Culture* 3.1 (2003) 83–108.

Marcuse, Herbert. *One Dimensional Man: Studies in the Ideology of Advanced Industrial Society*. London: Routledge, 2002.

Merleau-Ponty, Maurice. *Phenomenology of Perception*. New York: Routledge, 2012.

———. *Sense and Non-Sense*. Evanston, IL: Northwestern University Press, 1964.

———. *The Visible and the Invisible*. Evanston, IL: Northwestern University Press, 1968.

Milbank, John. *Theology and Social Theory: Beyond Secular Reason*. Oxford: Blackwell, 1990.

Morehead, John W. "Zombie Walks, Zombie Jesus and the Eschatology of Postmodern Flesh." In *The Undead and Theology*, edited by Kim Paffenroth and John Morehead, 101–23. Eugene, OR: Pickwick, 2012.

Moyse, Ashley John. "When All Is Lost, Gather 'Round: Solidarity as Hope Resisting Despair in 'The Walking Dead.'" In *The Undead and Theology*, 124–44. Eugene: Pickwick, 2012.

Mumford, Lewis. *The City in History*. Harmondsworth, UK: Penguin, 1961.

Paffenroth, Kim. "Apocalyptic Images and Prophetic Functions in Zombie Films." In *The Undead and Theology*, edited by Kim Paffenroth and John Morehead, 145–64. Eugene, OR: Pickwick, 2012.

Pickstock, Catherine. *After Writing: On the Liturgical Consummation of Philosophy*. Oxford: Blackwell, 1997.

Pieper, Josef. *Faith, Hope, Love*. San Francisco: Ignatius, 1997.

Pound, Marcus. *Žižek: A (Very) Critical Introduction*. Grand Rapids: Eerdmans, 2008.

Romero, George, *Night of the Living Dead*. Hollywood, CA: Market Square Productions, 1968.

Romero, George. *Dawn of the Dead*. Hollywood, CA: Laurel Group, 1978.

Saint, P. Michael, Robert J. Flavell, and Patrick F. Fox. *NIMBY Wars: The Politics of Land Use*. No loc: Saint University Press, 2009.

Schmemann, Alexander. *For the Life of the World*. New York: St. Vladimir's Seminary Press, 1973.

Shaviro, Steven. *The Cinematic Body*. Minneapolis: University of Minnesota Press, 1993.

Sigurdson, Ola. "Slavoj Žižek, the Death Drive, and Zombies: A Theological Account." *Modern Theology* 29.3 (2013) 361–80.

Tanner, Laura. *Intimate Violence: Reading Rape and Torture in Twentieth Century Fiction*. Bloomington, IN: Indiana University Press, 1994.

Turner, Bryan S. *The Body and Society*. 3rd ed. Los Angeles: Sage, 2008.

Ward, Graham. *Christ and Culture*. Oxford: Blackwell, 2005.

———. *Cities of God*. London: Routledge, 2000.

———. *The Politics of Discipleship*. The Church and Postmodern Culture. Grand Rapids: Baker Academic, 2009.

Wasserman, Renata R. Mautner. "The Self, the Mirror, the Other: 'The Fall of the House of Usher.'" *Poe Studies* 10.2 (1977) 33–35.

Žižek, Slavoj. *Did Somebody Say Totalitarianism? Five Interventions in the (Mis) Use of a Notion*. London: Verso, 2001.

———. *The Žižek Reader*. Edited by Elizabeth and Edmond Wright. Oxford: Blackwell, 1999.

Name Index

Name Index

Laderman, Gary, 19
Latour, Bruno, 4, 24
Le Corbusier, 21, 23
Loudermilk, A., 17, 19, 31, 45

Mailer, Norman, 43
Marcuse, Herbert, 30
Merleau-Ponty, Maurice, 60–61
Meyer, Stephanie (*Twilight*), 13
Morehead, John, 48–49
Moyse, Ashley, 53
Mumford, Lewis, 23

Neo (*The Matrix*), 27–28
Newsboys, 22

Paffenroth, Kim, 14, 17–18, 35, 54, 58n24
Parnell, Thomas, 10
Peletier, Carol (*The Walking Dead*), 68
Peter (*Dawn of the Dead*), 17
Pickstock, Catherine, 32–36, 39, 78, 83
Pieper, Josef, 68n52, 69
Pius IX, Pope, 80
Poe, Edgar Allen, 12–13
Pound, Marcus, 69n53, 79n15, 81n22

Red Skull, 29

Ritchie, Lionel, 22
Romero, George, 4, 14–17, 19–20, 45, 57, 67

Samuels, Lizzie (*The Walking Dead*), 68–69
Schmemann, Alexander, 58, 59, 70–71, 92
Shaviro, Steven, 18
Shelley, Mary, 12
Sigurdson, Ola, 26, 35, 50
Sprague, Eric, 29
Steele, Anastasia (*50 Shades of Grey*), 42
Stoker, Bram, 13

Tanner, Laura, 40, 43, 44n85
Turner, Bryan, 38n68

Wachowskis, The, 27
Ward, Graham, 4, 22–23, 25, 27, 28, 31, 34–35, 38–41, 43, 45, 52, 54–56, 59, 61–62, 66, 83
Warton, Joseph, 10
Warwick, Dionne, 22

X-men, 27

Žižk, Slavoj, 4, 26, 35, 49–52, 61, 79n14, 89, 90